The Best of Coaching Volleyball, Book III:
The Related Elements of the Game

Edited by Kinda S. Asher

A Division of Howard W. Sams & Co.
A Bell Atlantic Company

Published by Masters Press
(A Division of Howard W. Sams & Company, A Bell Atlantic Company)
2647 Waterfront Pkwy. E. Drive, Suite 300
Indianapolis, IN 46214

© 1996 American Volleyball Coaches Association

All Rights Reserved

Published 1996

Printed in the United States of America

No part of this publication may be reproduced, stored in a retrieval system or transmitted, in any form or by any means, electronic, mechanical, photocopying, recording or otherwise, without the prior permission of Masters Press.

Library of Congress Cataloging-in-Publication Data

The best of coaching volleyball series of handbooks/ American Volleyball Coaches Association.
    p.   cm.
   Includes bibliographical references and indexes.
   Contents: [1] Basic elements of the game -- [2] Advanced elements of the game [3] Related elements of the game.
   ISBN 1-57028-083-5 (v.1). -- ISBN 1-57028-084-3 (v.2). -- ISBN 1-57028-085-1 (v.3).
   1. Volleyball -- Coaching -- Handbooks, manuals, etc. I. American Volleyball Coaches Association.
II. Coaching volleyball.

GV1015.5.C63B47 1995   95-43827
796.325--dc20   CIP

The Best of Coaching Volleyball, Book III: The Related Elements of the Game

Credits:
Cover design by Dennis Kugizaki, Kugizaki Design Inc., Colorado Springs, Colo.
Text design by Kevin Kaneshiro, American Volleyball Coaches Association
Cover photo: Roger Mar
Cover coach: Pat Kendrick, head women's volleyball coach, George Mason University

Table of Contents

Acknowledgements ... ix

Preface ... x

Section I - Conditioning and Volleyball
- Chapter 1 - Year-Round Conditioning - Bob Alejo ... 1
- Chapter 2 - Plyometrics for Volleyball - Lori Alexander ... 7
- Chapter 3 - Plyometrics and Progress: A Case Study - Jodi Borkowski ... 11
- Chapter 4 - Training in Sand for More Powerful Legs - Istvan Javorek ... 15
- Chapter 5 - Movement Training - Fred Featherstone ... 19

Section II - Dealing with Injury
- Chapter 6 - Causes and Treatments of Muscle Cramps ... 25
- Chapter 7 - Psychological Ramifications for the Injured Athlete - Cynthia Booth ... 29

Section III - Psychology of Sport
- Chapter 8 - The Psychology of Optimal Volleyball: Teaching Mental Skills to Physical People - Nate Zinsser, Ph.D., and Robert Gambardella ... 37
- Chapter 9 - The Psychology of Optimal Volleyball: Effective Thinking - Nate Zinsser, Ph.D., and Robert Gambardella ... 43
- Chapter 10 - The Psychology of Optimal Volleyball: A New Look at Arousal and Performance - Nate Zinsser, Ph.D., and Robert Gambardella ... 49
- Chapter 11 - The Performance Dynamic: A Three-Stage Process - Nate Zinsser, Ph.D., and Robert Gambardella ... 55
- Chapter 12 - The Attentional Demands of Volleyball - Iradge Ahrabi-Fard, Ph.D., and Sharon Huddleston, Ph.D. ... 61
- Chapter 13 - Cue Recognition Training - Iradge Ahrabi-Fard, Ph.D., and Sharon Huddleston, Ph.D. ... 67
- Chapter 14 - Lessons for Coaches - Peter Hastie, Ph.D. ... 73
- Chapter 15 - Maximizing Your Leadership Style - Carol Gruber, Ph.D ... 77
- Chapter 16 - Momentum - Richard Bennett ... 81
- Chapter 17 - Teaching Skills Effectively - Lisa Kowalski ... 85

Section IV - Coaching Philosophy and Ethics
- Chapter 18 - Commandments for Volleyball Coaches - Karen Heinemann ... 91
- Chapter 19 - Coaches Should Keep Volleyball in Perspective - Renee De Graff ... 95
- Chapter 20 - Effective Communication - Karen Gee ... 99
- Chapter 21 - Communication Can Give You the Winning Edge - Lenore Suarez and I.J. Gorman ... 103
- Chapter 22 - Effective Timeout Communication - Walt Ker ... 107
- Chapter 23 - Finding Friends in Coaching - Marilyn McNeil, Ph.D. ... 113

Section V - Program Development/Management
        Chapter 24 - Home Events: More than a Game - Pam Bradetich   119
        Chapter 25 - Improving Your Team's Media Coverage - Dan Dittmer   125
        Chapter 26 - Increasing Your Volleyball Program's Income - Darlene Kluka, Ph.D.   129

Section VI - Statistics
        Chapter 27 - The Statistics Crew: Vital to Your Program - Grant Burger   133
        Chapter 28 - A Simple Statistical Program for High School Volleyball -
                Sid Feldman   137
        Chapter 29 - Recording Volleyball Statistics Easily: The Schroeder System -
                Lois Mueller   141
        Chapter 30 - Chart a Path to Success With the Total Performance Chart -
                Brett Mills and Mick Mack   145

Contributors

Authors

Iradge Ahrabi-Fard, Ph.D., head women's coach, University of Northern Iowa (Cedar Falls, Iowa)

Lori Alexander, C.S.C.S., certified strength and conditioning specialist, University of California, Berkeley

Bob Alejo, conditioning coach, The Oakland Athletics Baseball Company

Richard Bennett, head girls' volleyball coach, Heidelberg High School (Heidelberg, Germany)

Cynthia Boothe, MS, ATC, professor, HPE Department, Moorhead State University (Moorhead, Minn.)

*Jodi Borkowski, supervising student trainer, Beloit College (Beloit, Wis.)

*Pam Bradetich, former administrative assistant/events manager, Washington State University (Pullman, Wash.)

Grant Burger, former AVCA director of sports information

Renee De Graff, marketing specialist, Gordon Food Services

*Dan Dittmer, former head girls' volleyball coach, Chimacum High School (Chimacum, Wash.)

Fred Featherstone, head men's volleyball coach, Grossmont College (El Cajon, Calif.)

*Sid Feldman, former head women's volleyball coach, University of Georgia (Athens, Ga.)

Robert Gambardella, director, Youth Development and Programs, USA Volleyball

Karen Gee, president, Affiliated Boards of Officials

*I.J. Gorman, former assistant women's volleyball and strength coach, Principia College (Elsah, Ill.)

Carol Gruber, Ph.D., director, Student Services, University of Iowa (Iowa City, Iowa)

Peter Hastie, Ph.D., assistant professor, Department of Health and Human Performance, Auburn University (Auburn University, Ala.)

*Karen Heinemann, former head girls' volleyball coach, Southern High School (Durham, N.C.)

Sharon Huddleston, Ph.D., associate professor and sport psychologist, University of Northern Iowa

Istvan Javorek, all-sport conditioning supervisor, Johnson County Community College (Overland Park, Kan.)

*Walt Ker, former head women's volleyball coach, Cal State Northridge

Darlene Kluka, Ph.D., assistant professor, coordinator of Graduate Studies, University of Central Oklahoma (Edmond, Okla.)

Lisa Kowalski, head women's volleyball coach, Belleville Area College (Belleville, Ill.)

Marilyn McNeil, Ph.D., athletics director, Monmouth College (West Long Branch, N.J.)

Brett Mills, director of research, U.S. Sports Academy (Daphne, Ala.)

Mick Mack, sport psychology instructor, University of Northern Iowa

*Lois Mueller, former associate professor, Concordia University (Mequon, Wis.)

Lenore Suarez, head women's volleyball coach, Principia College (Elsah, Ill.)

Nate Zinsser, Ph.D., sport psychologist, U.S. Military Academy's Center for Enhanced Performance (West Point, N.Y.)

Editors

General Editor: Kinda Asher, director of publications, American Volleyball Coaches Association

Layout Assistant Editor: Gavin Markovits, intern, American Volleyball Coaches Association

Copy Editors: Sandra Vivas and Vivian Langley

Advisors

Darlene Kluka, Ph.D., assistant professor, University of Central Oklahoma

Sean Madden, head women's coach, Gonzaga University

Geri Polvino, Ph.D., head women's coach, Eastern Kentucky University

Don Shondell, Ph.D., head men's coach, Ball State University

Sandra Vivas, executive director, American Volleyball Coaches Association

*coaching position at the time the article was first published in *Coaching Volleyball*.

Acknowledgements

In today's world, the measure of true success is seen in the compilation. Professional musicians release "best of" CDs, while actors and actresses are judged by the body of their work, as are authors and researchers. Indeed, if a particular person, event or publication has been around long enough — and has been successful enough — to warrant a "collection," there is a demand for the product. Since 1987, there has been a demand for *Coaching Volleyball*, the official technical journal of the American Volleyball Coaches Association, and now the best the publication has to offer can be found in a new series of books.

The *Best of Coaching Volleyball* series (Books I-III) was the brainchild of the *Coaching Volleyball* Editorial Board and the AVCA office staff. The AVCA is continually searching for innovative avenues to serve its members from an educational standpoint; the *Best of Coaching Volleyball* series is one of the many innovations.

The project could not have begun without the *Coaching Volleyball* Editorial Board, specifically Darlene Kluka, Ph.D. (assistant professor, University of Central Oklahoma), Sean Madden (head women's volleyball coach, Gonzaga University), Geri Polvino, Ph.D. (head women's volleyball coach, Eastern Kentucky) and Don Shondell, Ph.D. (head men's volleyball coach, Ball State University), without whose expertise and patience this publication would have floundered. In addition, the AVCA membership itself must be praised, as it is the members of the organization — the coaches of all levels — who provide the articles for *Coaching Volleyball* on a consistent basis. Without their willingness to share ideas on this ever changing sport, the journal itself would not exist. The coaches who are also USA Volleyball Coaching Accreditation Program (CAP) participants strive continually to "shake up" the volleyball world with innovative new techniques and tactics.

Undeniably, the heartiest thanks must go to the 29 authors whose works appear in this publication. Revisions and fine tuning of these articles was a responsibility thrust upon them — and each took the challenge to heart.

Finally, many thanks go to Tom Bast, publisher, Holly Kondras, editor, and the rest of the Masters Press staff for their support and expertise throughout the varied stages of this project. The first two publications in the series, *The Best of Coaching Volleyball, Book One: The Basic Elements of the Game* and *The Best of Coaching Volleyball, Book Two: The Advanced Elements of the Game*, continue to enjoy phenomenal success. Undeniably, *Book Three* will uphold the tradition.

Kinda S. Asher
AVCA Director of Publications
May 1996

Preface

Eight years ago, the American Volleyball Coaches Association recognized the need for a technical journal specifically designed for volleyball coaches of all levels, from junior/club to international. As a result, *Coaching Volleyball* was born.

Today, *Coaching Volleyball* serves as the leading periodical devoted to the technical aspects of the game. The journal is read bi-monthly by more than 3,000 AVCA members and subscribers, both domestic and international. The demand for technically correct information on coaching and learning the sport has inspired the AVCA to compile the best articles from the technical journal and showcase them in a series of three publications. The *Best of Coaching Volleyball* series (Books I-III) is the response to that need.

In this, the third book of the series, coaches and players are treated to 30 chapters discussing the related elements of the game of volleyball. Authors from all disciplines -- and from all around the country -- offer their ideas on conditioning, dealing with injury, program development and coaching philosophy, to name just a few topics included in this publication. It is truly an eclectic combination of information geared to coaches and players, no matter the level of volleyball expertise.

The book is divided into six sections:

Section I	Conditioning and Volleyball
Section II	Dealing With Injury
Section III	Psychology of Sport
Section IV	Coaching Philosophy and Ethics
Section V	Program Development/Management
Section VI	Statistics

Twenty-nine authors have offered their varied expertise on the sport of volleyball. Each chapter is rife with photos, graphics and diagrams to aid the reader in understanding and grasping the material. In addition, a number of the chapters pull related information from other sources to provide the reader with an even broader base of information. Indeed, the *Best of Coaching Volleyball* series is unlike any volleyball publication you have read.

Kinda S. Asher, Editor
AVCA Director of Publications

Section I: Conditioning and Volleyball

Year-Round Conditioning

Year-Round Conditioning

Bob Alejo

The training program at any institution can be successful only if the coaching staff and the student/athletes support the conditioning coaches and program 100 percent and feel it is necessary to maintain a high level of play. If the members of a volleyball program are committed to the conditioning program, it can expand and progress to become specific for volleyball and at times personalized for each athlete. The following information can be used as a model in designing a yearly program at the collegiate level.

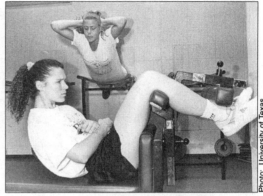

IN-SEASON TRAINING

The in-season or competitive training period begins in August with a summer program test. During the summer, athletes perform a training program on their own. Realistically, most athletes will find it difficult to get to the gym two to three times per week in the summer, so a menu of exercises is designed that can be performed anywhere, anytime to promote volleyball fitness. Table 1 lists these exercises and the progression of work performed.

If the members of a volleyball program are committed to the conditioning program, it can expand and progress to become specific for volleyball and at times personalized for each athlete.

TABLE 1 - Summer Training Program

Exercise/Date	6/25	7/2	7/9	7/16	7/23	7/30	8/6
Lunges	12	14	16	18	20	22	24
Push-ups	2x4	3x4	4x4	5x4	6x4	7x4	8x4
Squats	22	24	26	28	30	32	34
Lying Hyperextensions	12	14	16	18	20	22	24
Pause jumps	12	14	16	18	20	22	24
Double jumps	4	5	6	7	8	9	10
Stomach crunches	3x30	3x30	4x30	4x30	5x30	5x30	5x30
Lateral hops - 24" width	2x20	3x20	4x20	5x20	6x20	7x20	8x20
15-yd. sprints - 10-second interval	15	20	25	30	35	40	45

Explanation of Summer Program Exercise
Lunges - Listed repetitions for each leg while moving forward.
Push-ups - Take as much rest as needed to complete the sets. Do not do them consecutively even if you can.
Squats - Regular squat depth (90 degrees) with your hands clasped behind the head.
Lying hyperextensions - Lie face down on the floor with the hands clasped behind the head. Raise both the upper body and legs off of the ground and hold for two seconds. Do not jerk into the up position.
Pause jumps - Begin in the block ready position with the hands in the air. Squat down to 90 degrees, come to a complete stop, then explode vertically.
Double jumps - One set equals two consecutive max vertical jumps as quickly as possible.
Stomach crunches - Knees up, just raise the shoulder blades off the ground.
Lateral hops - Measure off 24 inches. With both feet, jump back and forth over the line, maintaining good balance. Every time you come back to the start it counts as one repetition.
15-yard sprints - Make sure you are running 15 yards; you will be tested at this distance. Only take 10 seconds of rest. You will be tested at this interval.

When the players return in August, their commitment to the program is determined by administering a sprint/interval test. This test has no time standard other than the set interval. The athletes are evaluated by watching them run the test shoulder to shoulder and noting fatigue, inten-

Leg presses help the athlete to work immediately on leg strength with little attention to technique.

sity and discipline. A training staff member's evaluation of the test will also give the coaches an idea of what to expect in practice.

Following the test, the four-day-per-week in-season workout begins. This in-season cycle precedes the beginning of classes. On days one and three, free weight training combined with selectorized weight stack (pin-type) machines and six fitness-type exercises are done. The free weight program is designed to work on strength and power, while the circuit is for endurance and joint fitness.

Ideally, never try to train more than one major quality in one cycle. If a program is designed to elicit power in the athlete, one cannot expect to optimize strength or endurance. This statement appears to contradict the first cycle program objectives. Because there are only three to four weeks for this cycle of training, this mixed approach accomplishes a crash course in weight training. In this instance, a broad approach is wanted. Table 2 lists this first cycle's exercises.

The second cycle of in-season training begins after the first match of the year. At that time, the athlete trains two times per week for about 30 to 45 minutes. The desired goal is to be around 85 percent of the spring 1 RM (repetition maximum) in the bench press and pulling movements and about 60 percent on pause squats. At 85 per-

TABLE 2 - Sample of In-Season Training Program

Cycle 1	Sets x Repetitions
Lateral Box Hops (R)	2x10
Good Morning/Push Press (R)	1x10 (warm-up)
	3x5
Clean Deadlift (F)	1x10 (warm-up)
	3x5
Clean Pull (R)	1x5 (warm-up)
	4x3
Back Squat w/three-count Pause (R)	1x10 (warm-up)
	4x3
Bench Press (F/R)	1x10 (warm-up)
	4x3 (R)
	3x5 (F)
Hyperextension (F/R)	3x5 (add weight and hold)
Leg Press (F)	1x10 (warm-up)
	3x5
Lunges (F)	3x5 (use bar)
Leg Extension (R)	4x12 w/20 seconds rest
	(last 20-30 degrees of extension only)
Eagle Leg Curls (**) (F)	4x8
Eagle Leg Extensions (**) (F)	2x8
Upright Rows (F)	2x6
Dumbell Pullover (R/F)	2x6 (F)
	3x5 (R)
Lat Pulldowns (F)	2x6
Hyper Sit-ups (F)	3x10
Rotator Cuff Series (R)	
Internal/external rotation	1x20
Empty can	1x20
Opposite can	1x20
Arm circles	2x10
Seated Calf Raise (R/F)	2x8
	2x15
Cycle 2	**Sets x Time**
Kill Circuit (*)	
Squat Military	3x 10 seconds
Chest Press Leg Curl	for each exercise
Pause Squat Medicine Ball	
Pause Hypers Leg Extension (hold)	(allow 20 seconds
Upper Back Lateral Hops (6")	rest between intervals)
Torso Curls Ankle Circuit	

Note: Athlete will count her own reps.

Explanation of In-Season Training Program
Subject - Returning players (R) and Incoming Freshmen (F)
Program Design - This menu of exercises is a sample program for returning players and incoming freshmen in the fall. This three- to four-week cycle is to be used during the preseason only. Once competition starts, discontinue the Cycle 2 workout. Remember, adjustments are continually made in the workout for each athlete based on his/her needs, progress, injuries, fatigue, etc.
Workout Schedule - The program is a four-day-per-week workout. Cycle 1 should be done on Day 1 and Day 3; Cycle 2 should be done on Day 2 and Day 4.
(**) *Eagle* - Eagle is a brand name of equipment used in the exercise. (*) *Kill Circuit* - Kill is a brand name of the equipment used in the exercise.

cent, the weight is heavy enough for strength increases or maintenance, but the repetitions are low enough so that fatigue will not affect the athlete's volleyball skills.

To allow for mid-season fatigue, the program has a reduction in repetitions and is performed in an alternating heavy/light format. Training is heavy the first bout of the week and is reduced between 30 to 40 percent for the second bout. The repetitions are the same for both bouts.

Freshman athletes, unless they are full-time players, continue to train heavy both days of training with higher repetitions than the returning athletes. The only pulling movement is the clean deadlift and leg press is used instead of back squats. This represents the basic training that must be implemented for the untrained athlete to make the proper progress through the years. The deadlift teaches the athlete correct technique from the ground to the hip, which is so necessary for efficient pulling. Leg presses help the freshman athlete to work immediately on leg strength with little attention to technique. The author considers the winter to be the most productive time for teaching technique in the squats and pulls. The freshman program begins with low repetitions and builds as the season continues. This satisfies two major needs:

1) when beginning with high repetitions, fatigue becomes a deterrent to effective learning of new movements, so roughly the same poundages are maintained throughout the season, but increase the repetitions;

2) once the athlete learns the movement, it is repetition that will commit the execution to memory, while the athlete gains weight training fitness.

Throughout the year, but most importantly during the season, workouts need to be modified due to injury, illness, fatigue or scheduling.

OFF-SEASON WINTER

Getting back into weight training fitness as soon as possible after the regular season is highly recommended because the winter is a great time to lay the foundation for more specific work in the spring.

In a four-week cycle, the athletes start at low repetitions and build to a difficult fourth week. Following this, a simple descending reps form for

TABLE 3 - Sample of Winter Training Program

Exercise	Day	Sets x Repetitions
Push Press (R/F)	Tu, Th	1x5 (warm-up)
		3x4
Back Squat (R/F)	Tu, Th	1x10 (warm-up)
		3x6
		1x5 (pause)
Clean Pulls (R/F)	Tu, Th	3x3 (warm-up) (F)
		1x10 (warm-up) (R)
		3x5
Clean Deadlift (R/F)	Tu, Th	3x5 (R)
		5x5 (F)
		4x3
Good Mornings (R)	Tu, Th	3x6
Hyperextension (F)	Tu, Th	3x8 (use weight and hold)
Bench Press (R/F)	Tu, Th	1x10 (warm-up)
		3x4
Dumbbell Incline Press (R/F)	Tu, Th	2x12 (R)
		2x8 (F)
Dumbbell Pullover (R/F)	Tu, Th	2x12 (R)
		2x8 (F)
Upper Back (Eagle/Kill) (R/F)	Tu, Th	2x12 (R)
		2x8 (F)
Barbell Curl (R/F)	Tu, Th	2x12 (R)
		2x8 (F)
Lying Tricep (R/F)	Tu, Th	2x12 (R)
		2x8 (F)
Leg Curl (Eagle/Kill) (R/F)	Tu, Th	4x8
Leg Extension (Eagle/Kill) (R/F)	Tu, Th	2x15 (R)
		2x12 (F)
Seated Calf Raises (R/F)	Tu, Th	2x15 (R)
		2x12 (F)
Rotator Cuff Series (R)		
Empty can	Tu, Th	1x20
Opposite can	Tu, Th	1x20
Lying extension	Tu, Th	1x20
Arm circles	Tu, Th	2x20
Hyper Sit-ups (R/F)	Tu, Th	2x20
		2x15

Explanation of Winter Training Program
Subjects - Returning Players (R) and Incoming Freshmen (F)
Program Design - This menu of exercises is a sample program for returning players and the freshmen in the winter.
Workout Schedule - The program is a four-week, two-day-per-week workout. The athletes start at low repetitions and build to a difficult fourth week.

TABLE 4 - Sample Spring Training Program

Exercise	Day	Week 1	Week 2	Week 3	Week 4
Push Press	Tues.	1x5 (warm-up)	1x5	1x5	1x5
		3x5 (same weight)	3x5	3x5	3x5
Good Morning	Thur.	1x5 (warm-up)	1x5	1x5	1x5
		3x5 (same weight)	3x5	3x5	3x5
Power Clean	Tues.	1x5 (warm-up)	1x5	1x5	1x5
		4x3 (70%)	4x3 (75%)	4x2 (80%)	4x3 (80%)
Clean Pulls	Thurs.	1x5 (warm-up)	1x5	1x5	1x5
		4x3 (85%)	4x5 (85%)	4x3 (90%)	4x4 (90%)
Back Squat	Tues.	1x10 (warm-up)	1x10	1x10	1x10
		3x8 (70%)	3x8 (75%)	3x5 (80%)	3x5 (85%)
Back Squat	Thur.	1x10 (warm-up)	1x10	1x10	1x10
		3x5 (60%)	3x5 (65%)	4x3 (65%)	4x3 (65%)
Good Morning, bent leg	Tues.	3x5	3x5	3x5	3x5
Bench Press	Tues.	1x10 (warm-up)	1x10	1x10	1x10
		3x5 (75%)	3x8 (75%)	3x5 (80%)	3x5 (85%)
Bench Press	Thur.	1x10 (warm-up)	1x10	1x10	1x10
		3x5 (75%)	3x8 (75%)	3x3 (70%)	3x5 (75%)
Dumbbell Incline Press	Both	2x6	2x6	2x6	2x6
Dumbbell Pullover	Both	2x6	2x6	2x6	2x6
Upper Back (Eagle/Kill)	Both	2x6	2x6	2x6	2x6
Barbell Curl	Both	2x6	2x6	2x6	2x6
Lying Tricep	Both	2x6	2x6	2x6	2x6
Leg Curl (Eagle/Kill)	Both	4x5	4x5	4x5	4x5
Leg Extension	Both	2x12	2x12	2x12	2x12
Seated Calf Raise	Both	2x12	2x12	2x12	2x12
Rotator Cuff Series					
Empty Can (1.25 kg)	Both	1x20	1x20	1x20	1x20
Opposite Can (1.25 kg)	Both	1x20	1x20	1x20	1x20
Lying Extension (1.25 kg)	Both	1x20	1x20	1x20	1x20
Arm Circles (1.25 kg)	Both	2x10	2x10	2x10	2x10
Hyper Sit-ups	Both	2x45	2x50	2x55	2x60

Explanation of Spring Training Program
Subjects - All players on team.
Program Design - This menu of exercises is a sample program for all players in the spring.
Workout Schedule - The program is a two-day-per-week workout.

the bench press and back squats is implemented and the repetitions in the supplemental exercises are decreased. The freshmen athletes increase repetitions on the supplemental exercises to continue to lay a good first-year base (see Table 3).

A plyometric program begins the second week of weight training and is primarily composed of single response exercises. The athletes train laterally, horizontally and vertically to cover all of the basic volleyball movements. Following the eight-week weight training program, the 1 RM in the bench press and back squat for each athlete is tested. Vertical jump testing includes the no-step jump and the three-step approach. Body composition is measured by a hand-held tester called a Skyndex.

The desired goal is to equal the previous spring's strength and power tests. Nevertheless, this is not true all the time, especially with the older athletes. Due to the difference in the training objectives of the four seasons, coaches should not always expect linear progress. For example, it might be more logical to compare the results of the older athletes on a year-to-year basis per lift. Younger athletes will most likely progress cycle-to-cycle due to their level of training, but at some point will level off or show decreasing results. Prior to this time, individualizing the training cycle must be undertaken so the athletes can attain the optimal level. Past experiences have proven that springtime is best for a program change.

OFF-SEASON SPRING

The length of the spring program is the same as the winter, but the objectives are entirely different. In this phase, the athletes are training to reach the highest results in the jump testing; subsequently, the other test scores will show an increase due to the low volume/high intensity mode of training. Regardless of the level of the athlete or the winter test scores, the athlete should always have the highest test results during this period.

As stated earlier, spring is a preferred time to get specific to each athlete's needs. Based on the specific quality being trained, there could be as many as seven different programs. The ideal situation would be a heavy/light program with advanced combination speed/strength movements and advanced plyometrics taking up the majority of the training time. This would mean that adequate upper and lower body strength has been achieved and the ultimate application of that strength into power becomes the entire focus. Table 4 shows an example of one spring program. Notice the change in intensity from workout to workout.

During the winter program, plyometrics are performed after the training session. Due to the necessity of speed for the proper execution of plyometric exercises, training induced fatigue would normally be contraindicated. During this preparatory phase of training, this will have a positive effect on jumping fitness. The plyometric movements at this time are low level, so the chance for injury due to fatigue is minimal. As in a volleyball match, the athlete is asked to jump with the presence of fatigue and this is where this response mechanism can be trained. Just the opposite is true for the spring program. Jumping occurs prior to training for three reasons:

- the jumps are multi-response and cannot be effectively performed when fatigued;
- we are trying to optimize jumping results, so we train our priority first; and
- speed-oriented movements this complicated should be done early in the training session.

> The length of the spring program is the same as the winter, but the objectives are entirely different. In this phase, the athletes are training to reach the highest results in the jump testing; subsequently, the other test scores will show an increase due to the low volume/high intensity mode of training.

SUMMARY

This general overview of an effective conditioning program should serve as a reference when designing programs for your own situation. Copying a program would be of little benefit, unless your training environment is identical to that of the design in question. Instead, extract a philosophy and build upon it. In summary, the program's philosophy contains these points:

1) Emphasize low back, glute, hamstring and quadricep training.
2) Train with volleyball-specific plyometrics, but be conservative.
3) Try to individualize all programs.
4) Use rotator cuff conditioning for preventative measures.
5) Work toward speed/strength training and less pure strength training. Power is the best application to sport.
6) Basic training should be employed for the freshman athlete for at least six months.

Bob Alejo is the conditioning coach for the Oakland Athletics Baseball Company.

Plyometrics for Volleyball

Plyometrics for Volleyball

LORI ALEXANDER

When designing a strength and conditioning program for volleyball, it is important to focus on increasing explosive power in the athletes as well as increasing strength, improving performance and preventing injuries. This can be accomplished through a combination of strength training and plyometrics.

A strength training program providing a general strength base should precede any specialized program. When a strength base has been established, a more specific program can be initiated. A strength program consisting of the basic lifts as well as several multi-joint exercises such as cleans and push jerks, should be continued after a four to six-week general program. Exercises should include the range of motion used in volleyball. Squats (front and back), step ups, lunges, leg presses, leg extensions, leg curls, glute/ham raises and heel raises will ensure proper preparation for plyometric workouts.

Squats (front and back) lunges, leg presses, leg extensions, leg curls, glute/ham raises and heel raises will ensure proper preparation for plyometric workouts.

A strong trunk is also important. For total body power, exercises such as twisting sit-ups, crunches, twists, Russian twists, good mornings and back extensions will improve midsection strength. Including medicine ball workouts in the general program is excellent for improving trunk strength, stability and increasing upper body power.

$$\text{Power} = \frac{\text{Force} \times \text{Time}}{\text{Distance}}$$

The athlete needs to focus on power, speed and explosiveness more than lifting maximal weight. Explosive power is the most strength that can be applied in the shortest amount of time. The formula for power is force (or strength) multiplied by time divided by distance. Since distance is not a variable in volleyball, the formula shows that power can be increased by either increasing strength or decreasing reaction time.

When starting a plyometric program, as with strength training, a general base program should precede more difficult and specific workouts. The plyometric program should begin with simple standing hops, then progress to box jumps, multiple jumps and depth jumps. The key to a successful plyometric program is focusing on quality, not quantity. Each repetition of each set of each exercise should be an all-out maximal effort. Keeping the number of sets and repetitions at a minimum and allowing proper recovery between sets will help ensure that the quality and intensity of effort will remain maximal. This will also help reduce the risk of injury due to fatigue.

The following exercises progress from beginning jumps to more difficult and complex exercises. All jumps should be executed on a forgiving surface such as grass or synthetic floors for beginning jumps. Box

The purpose of plyometrics or jump training is to reduce contact time with the ground by training the stretch shortening cycle, i.e., landing, transfer and jumping.

According to Dan McDonough, USA Volleyball sports medicine coordinator, "One of the most important things about plyometrics is the players have to rest very well between sets. Some of the players we have who come in from colleges perform plyometrics that look like an aerobics class. Plyometrics are not aerobics. You can only do a limited number of them. The highest we ever go with the national team is 10 reps and with bounds we only go 30 feet. That can vary with what you are trying to get to, but that is standard."

"When I think about the patterns that a setter runs in a game -- penetrating from serve receive, going to cover, going back to defense, coming back in to set -- she is running all over the court. In the course of a five-game match, you have probably run a couple of miles. You have to be quick and accurate the whole time."

(McDonough, Dan. Power, agility and jumping enhancement. *Critical Thinking on Setter Development*, 1995, 48.)

jump and depth jumps require a softer gymnastic or wrestling mat for landing and rebounding.

BEGINNING JUMPS

• *Double Leg Hops*: Hop, rebounding quickly. May be done while moving forward or in place.

• *Ankle Flip*: Keeping the knee straight, step forward with the right foot. Push off the right foot using ankle extension only. Movement will be limited, but the foot should come off of the ground. Repeat with the left foot.

• *Skip for Height*: Skip using the knee. Drive with full extension off of the back foot. Go for height, not distance.

• *Bounding*: Stride forward, driving the knees up and/or out as far as possible using ankle flip and opposite arm drive.

• *Standing Long Jump/ Power Jump*: Jump with both feet while driving arms forward. Jump as far forward as possible.

• *Double Leg Hops with 180-Degree Turn*: Same as Double Leg Hops except for 180-degree turn between landings. Shoulders should be square at landing.

INTERMEDIATE JUMPS

• *Single Leg Hops*: Hop, rebounding quickly on one leg. Repeat with other leg. May be done while moving forward or in place.

• *Tuck Jumps*: Jump while tucking the knees up in front of the body, keeping the chest high and arms up.

• *Frog Leaps*: Squat with the hands between the legs on floor. Jump upward, achieving full extension. May be done for height or distance.

• *Split Lunge Jumps*: (Start in the lunge position.) Jump and land in a lunge position. Keep both knees at a 90-degree angle. May be done with a single leg or alternately.

• *Zig-Zag Jumps*: Using parallel lines approximately 2 to 3 feet apart, place right foot one line and hop forward and across to opposite line, landing on the right foot. Repeat with the left foot. Continue 10-20 yards.

• *Square Jumps*: Using intersecting lines on floor, hop (using one or both feet) in a square pattern as quickly as possible. Go both clockwise and counterclockwise.

• *Lateral Jumps*: Using parallel lines approximately 3 feet apart, stand with both feet on one line. Jump to the opposite line and return as quickly as possible. Repeat desired number of times.

• *Net Jumps*: Stand facing the net with arms up. Jump as high as possible, reaching up and over net. May be done opposite a partner on the other side of the net.

BOX JUMPS

• *Bench Push Offs*: Stand facing a 2-foot bench or box. Place one foot on the bench/box whith the leg at a 90-degree angle. Place the body

weight on the bent leg and push up and off the bench/box. Get as much height off of the box as possible. The exercise can be done landing on the same leg or alternate legs.
- *Single Box Jump*: Stand facing a box; jump up onto box with both feet. Can be done in sets of 10 to 15 or for a timed interval.
- *Multiple Box Jump With Stutter*: Stand facing a box; take off with both feet and jump completely over box. Stutter jump between boxes.
- *Multiple Box Jump*: Same as above without stutter jump. Immediate explosion upon landing. Can be done laterally as well as forward.

Above Box Jumps can be done with a single leg after double leg jumps have been mastered. This is for advanced athletes only.

DEPTH JUMPS
- *Single Depth Jump*: Step off of a box, landing on both feet; explode up immediately.
- *Double Depth Jump*: Same as single depth jump, except athlete continues to second box. Height of second box can be varied according to athlete's ability. Same as above, but jump completely over second box.
- *Multiple Depth Jumps*: Same as double depth jump, except using several boxes in a row.

On the above multiple jumps, boxes should not be placed far apart. Emphasis should be on increasing vertical power rather than horizontal. Bend as little as possible on landings.

CONCLUSION

The overall plyometric program should progress slowly. It is important to establish a solid strength base before beginning any jump exercises. Do not rush athletes through beginning jumps to the more advanced ones too quickly. Master double jumps before moving to single leg jumps. Plyometric workouts should be done two or three times a week on alternating days (T-Th, M-W-F). Do jump training before weight training in the workouts. Box height can be increased during the program to increase intensity level. The beginning height should be set at 1 to 3 feet and should not exceed 4 to 5 feet at the advanced level.

The program should consist of six-week cycles, with the last cycle ending a week or two before the season begins. Muscles can require up to two weeks to fully recover from heavy plyometric training. Lower intensity plyometrics can be incorporated into the competitive season.

Lori Alexander, C.S.C.S., is a certified strength and conditioning specialist at the University of California, Berkeley.

Six-Week Sample Program

Week 1/Exercise	Sets/Reps
Beginning Jumps - 4 exer.	2-3x8-10 reps
Intermediate Jumps - 4 exer.	3x8-12

Week 2/Exercise	Sets/Reps
Beginning Jumps - 2 exer.	2x8-10 reps
Intermediate Jumps - 4 exer.	3x8-12
Single Box Jumps	3x8

Week 3/Exercise	Sets/Reps
Beg./Intermediate Jumps - 4 exer.	2 sets
Single Box Jumps	2x8
Bench Push Offs	2x8 right
	2x8 left
Multiple Box Jumps w/ Short Hop	3x5 boxes

Week 4/Exercise	Sets/Reps
Beg./Intermediate Jumps - 4 exer.	2 sets
Bench Push Offs	2x12 alternating
Multiple Box Jumps	4x5 boxes
Single Depth Jumps	2x5

Week 5/Exercise	Sets/Reps
Beg./Intermediate Jumps - 4 exer.	1 set
Multiple Box Jumps	2x5 boxes
Single Depth Jumps	2x5
Double Depth Jumps	2x3-5 boxes

Week 6/Exercise	Sets/Reps
Beg/Intermediate Jumps - 4 exer.	1 set
Multiple Box Jumps	2x5 boxes
Single Depth Jumps	2x5
Multiple Depth Jumps	2x5 boxes

Plyometrics and Progress: A Case Study

Plyometrics and Progress: A Case Study

JODI BORKOWSKI

On the third day of preseason volleyball practice 15 very sore players wandered into the training room seeking a cure for their pain. Heat, ice and whirlpool treatments soothed their muscles only temporarily. As they climbed the stairs toward the gym, their soreness returned. Throughout practice, players were hesitant and slow, concentrating on their pain rather than on volleyball.

Wasting preseason teaching time to manage muscle soreness is a coach's nightmare. Until recently, preseason soreness was assumed to be unavoidable. However, the incorporation of an effective plyometric exercise into a preseason conditioning program can help decrease the pain felt in the early stages of the workout. (The primary reason to engage in a plyometrics program is to improve jump performance; however, muscle soreness reduction can be a secondary outcome.)

Depth Jumps

Illustrations courtesy of Performance Conditioning for Volleyball

PLYOMETRICS

Plyometric exercises are characterized by quick and powerful countermovements (eccentric muscle contractions followed by concentric contractions of the same muscles). One cause of muscle soreness is theorized to be created by the tearing of muscle cells resulting from eccentric contractions, which occur when a muscle lengthens while being contracted. For example, in a downhill sprint, the quadricep muscle group contracts as the leg is pulled upward and lengthens with each downward motion. Almost everyone—even the well-trained athlete—is sore after eccentric exercise. Michael Orendurff (1988) suggested that subjects are less susceptible to new soreness for up to six weeks after performing a single bout of eccentric exercise designed to cause muscle soreness. So although we probably cannot actually prevent muscle soreness, we can influence when we actually become resistant to it.

> Muscle soreness is theorized to be caused by the tearing of muscle cells resulting from eccentric contractions, which occur when a muscle lengthens while being contracted.

The following results from a modified version of Orendurff's plyometric exercise program show the great benefits of preseason conditioning. During preseason, the players performed three one-hour sessions of all-out eccentric exercise on designated days six, four and two weeks before the start of preseason practice (for advanced players only):
- five sets of five push-ups;
- six 40-yard downhill sprints (3-5° slope);
- four sets of eight depth jumps (18"-30");
- five sets of eight skips (similar to one-foot takeoff spike approaches);
- five sets of 10 lunges; and
- five sets of 10 lateral bounds.

The program was explained fully to team members and at the beginning of the summer they were sent descriptions and illustrations of each exercise, as well as a calendar outlining the plyometric exercise days. Nine out of 11 players participated in

Lateral Bounds

Lunges

the plyometric exercise program and most followed it precisely. (A few players deviated from the downhill sprints and ran on a flat surface because they did not have access to a hill with a 10-20° slope.)

The program's impact was immediately apparent upon the players' return to school. During preseason the players did not come to the training room for treatment of sore muscles: They stopped by just to talk. They ran up the stairs and in practice moved quickly and decisively. Most importantly, however, their concentration was on volleyball. According to Tami Falkenberg, a co-captain and starting middle hitter, "The plyometric program allowed us to be intense both physically and mentally right from the start."

As the team's trainer, I got a lot of positive feedback from the players. On the second, third and fourth days of twice-a-day practice (when preseason soreness usually hits hardest), many players excitedly proclaimed that they felt great. Others tentatively stated, "I am still not sore yet," almost afraid they might jinx their good fortune. At the onset of the regular season, players were asked to rate their preseason soreness for last year and the present year. The scale ranged from 1 to 5, with 1 indicating no soreness and 5 indicating extreme soreness. Last year's preseason received a median score of 4 (uncomfortable, entire body) and this year's a median score of 2 (minimal, restricted to specific areas). The neck and lower back were most commonly still subject to preseason soreness.

Head coach Pam Samuelson said the plyometric exercise program made a big impact on her team. It affected the way she planned practice because players could accomplish more without the bother of painful muscles. It greatly contributed to the team's progress, she said, because she was able to get the most out of the players in preseason, both physically and mentally. Evaluating the program's worth, Betsy Phinney, a starting middle hitter, summed up the team's attitude best: "It was only three days for an hour and the amount [of soreness] it prevented was 10 times that."

Used in conjunction with a summer conditioning program, a plyometric exercise program can produce desirable results, whereby athletes can come to preseason camp resistant to muscle soreness.

This was not a scientific study with control and experimental groups. It was merely a pilot test of a potentially beneficial program. Plyometrics' safety, specifically in landing techniques, has been criticized. And I do not know how much of the program's benefit is physiological and how much is psychological. Nevertheless, used in conjunction with a summer conditioning program, our plyometric exercise program produced desirable results. Athletes came to preseason camp resistant to muscle soreness. The program had a tremendous impact on the actions and attitudes of a competitive volleyball team.

SUGGESTED READINGS

Orendurff, M. Preventing muscle soreness. *Coaching Volleyball*, October/November 1988, 28-29.

Radcliffe, J. Producing power through plyometrics. *Coaching Volleyball*, December/January 1988, 12-15.

*Jodi Borkowski is a former supervising student trainer at Beloit College (Beloit, Wis.).

Training in Sand for More Powerful Legs

Training in Sand for More Powerful Legs

ISTVAN JAVOREK

The Brazilian national soccer teams in the 1960s were flexible and very explosive when jumping, sprinting, changing directions and starting. One of the reasons for that flexibility and explosiveness was that they practiced on sand. In the United States, many volleyball teams also practice and play on sand.

Because of the apparent success of training in sand, sand stairs and a sand volleyball court were built for training athletes at Johnson County Community College (Overland Park, Kan.). By training athletes in sand, the same explosive qualities can be developed. This article explains how sand stairs are built, the benefits of training in sand and a list of drills and exercises for sand.

The sand stairs are very simple to build and are generally inexpensive. The stairs are made of 2" x 10" lumber with rounded edges to minimize shin injuries. The stairs should be 3 to 5 feet in height and 2 to 3 feet in depth. The height and depth of each stair should be about 19 inches (also the depth of the sand). The number of stairs depends on need and available space.

Flexibility, strength and explosiveness are all benefits of training in the sand.

The greatest benefit of the sand stairs is the development of the explosive qualities of leg muscles, primarily through enhanced motor unit recruitment. In addition, it is an injury-free method of training. Because sand is a soft surface, the pressure on the tendons is minimal in the landing and take-off phases. In the landing, the amortization phase is longer and in the take-off, the difficulty is greater than on a normal jumping surface. The muscle receptors receive the stretch information later, which requires the athletes to concentrate more during the so-called "touch-and-go" phase. This long amortization phase stimulates the brain and spinal cord to greater temporal muscle fiber recruitment. This results in more of the available muscle fibers being involved due to this special recruitment, but they are still not strong enough to do the rebounding (in this situation). For this reason, a large number of muscle fibers are stimulated at a higher frequency (temporal recruitment). Both the longer amortization phase and the more difficult take-off contribute to improve the athlete's explosive qualities.

The following is a list of exercises for sand stairs:
- running up and down;
- running up with cross steps;
- jumping up and down facing up, right or left, right or left;
- consecutive single-leg bounding facing forward, right or left; right shoulder up, using left leg; left shoulder up, using left leg; left shoulder up, using right leg;
- consecutive double-leg depth jump facing forward, right or left; and
- consecutive single-leg depth jump facing forward, right or left; right shoulder down, using right leg; right shoulder down, using left leg; left shoulder down, using right leg.

The sand volleyball court has many of the same benefits as sand stairs. The sand court is good for developing fast and explosive leg muscles, plus cardiovascular conditioning can also

Sand stairs are very simple to build and generally inexpensive.

The greatest benefit of the sand stairs is the development of the explosive qualities of leg muscles.

be achieved. Bouncing, bounding, hopping and variations can be performed on a sand court.

When implementing sand training programs, pay close attention to the principles regarding intensity: easier drills before more intense drills (specific warm-up) and simple drills before complex, technical drills. After teaching athletes techniques, exercise on the normal stairs and after sufficient strength base is developed, start working on the sand stairs.

When beginning training on sand stairs, athletes should rest more between sets and gradually add more exercises, more reps and more sets. After a few weeks of preparation, increase the intensity by combining exercises and executing them in non-stop supersets. The superset usually contains three to five exercises. Start three exercises, two sets each and progress up to eight sets of each. The general conditioning level of the team determines the number of exercises and sets in a given workout. Set a goal of establishing a high level of physical conditioning by performing eight sets of five exercises in the superset. Exercises for the superset are:

- double-leg bounding x 2, gradually increasing to eight;
- double-leg take-off(up)—double-leg jump (down), one, two or three steps and spring x 2, gradually increasing to eight. This exercise is usually done up the stairs, turning back down the stairs (executing depth jumps down) and then sprint;
- single-leg bounding x 2, 4, 6 and 8, alternating legs each set. (Caution: when performing single-leg bounding, do not increase the number of sets before the athlete's work capacity is sufficient to maintain proper technique);
- double-leg sideward bounding x 2, 4, 6, 8 (left and right in alternating order); and
- sprint up the sand stairs x 2, working up to eight sets. As a general rule, do not let the athletes jump or land on the wooden frame of the stairs. They must jump into the box.

Continually vary the workouts, doing different combinations and supersets. The intensity and length of daily workouts will depend upon the goals and objectives for each day and training period. Always keep in mind that the sand stairs and court are just part of a total conditioning program, not an end in and of itself. On weights, the sandbox training can be more extensive.

SUMMARY

Always look for exercises and activities specific to the respective sports. Use exercise combinations for the general conditioning and basic volleyball movements requiring explosiveness of the legs and trunk. If you have the space and resources to construct sand stairs or a court, the training results will be quite positive.

Istvan Javorek is the all-sport conditioning supervisor for Johnson County Community College in Overland Park, Kansas.

Movement Training

Movement Training

FRED FEATHERSTONE

As volleyball evolves into a faster game with more specialization, players must be quicker at all levels of competition. In addition, athletes should strive to increase their physical range and the ability to travel longer distances linearly, laterally and vertically to play the ball.

Volleyball players are learning how to attack the volleyball at the net, out of the backcourt and in the serving zone with more efficiency, velocity and control than ever before. Hence, the coach's ability to develop quickness, explosive power and movement efficiently in players is paramount to success.

As a coach who has trained players at every level of competition, I am convinced that speed building and movement training are as important as technical skills training. Also, videotaping young players from the waist down while they are competing and practicing has validated my thinking about the importance of quickness and agility training. Most young players lack explosion, speed, fluidity and good anticipation.

The key for the coach is to acquire an understanding of how to improve. The various components of movement while training their players individually and the team collectively.

First, attention must be paid to anatomical function and joint stability when training an athlete physically. Next, emphasis must be placed on good balance and correct posture in movements prior to, during and following ball contact when conducting on-court training. Finally, without sacrificing range of motion and efficiency in movement, coaches need to help improve the physical parameters of strength, agility, quickness and explosive power in their athletes.

Players are learning to attack the ball at the net, out of the backcourt and in the serving zone with more efficiency, velocity and control than ever before. Therefore, the coach's ability to develop quickness, explosive power and movement efficiently in players is paramount to success.

Many young players initiate movement with their upper bodies rather than with their hips and legs. They are often late getting "a jump" on the ball and/or, conversely, may have a tendency to overplay the ball. Both girls and boys alike must be taught early how to move to the ball, reach for the ball, go through the ball, jump to the ball and react away from the ball. Players must also be trained to cut the ball off at the correct angle, how to move from point A on the court to point B and to recover and continue the play.

Footwork must be taught early: left-right movements, lunge movements, shuffle steps, running steps, cross-over steps, pivot steps and closing steps. The young volleyball player must be taught how and when to discriminate which specific movement is most appropriate for various situations on the court. In volleyball, the athlete's first two to three steps are usually the most important. Players must have the ability to start quickly and change direction. Slow, clumsy players will be unable to participate effectively.

> The young volleyball player must be taught how and when to discriminate which specific movement is most appropriate for various situations on the court. In volleyball, the athlete's first two to three steps are usually the most important. Players must have the ability to start quickly and change direction. Slow, clumsy players will be unable to participate effectively.

Finally, the coach must pay close attention to body-to-ball relationships, player spatial relationships, contact surfaces with the ball, coordination of adjoining positions, timing, elevation movements and emergency movements. In essence, knowing how to teach and improve movement is a complex job for the coach. To assist the coach in developing a module for movement training, a flow chart has been constructed to illustrate the various principles, prerequisites and progressions that apply to movement training (see Figure1).

In analyzing the flow chart, it is clear that certain physical and mental properties of the athlete are primary to improving movement efficiency. Indeed, top performance does not tolerate physical dysfunction. A player must possess good muscle function and joint stability before one can expect or demand an improvement in speed or quickness. An athlete must also be mentally focused and possess an aggressive, pursuit-minded attitude. There are a plethora of techniques and ways to improve a player's range, quickness, agility, functional strength and explosive power. The coach must construct a program that fits the level of competition and maturation of the athlete, time constraints for practicing, budget, etc.

Movement training is not merely developing quickness and explosion. It involves constant feedback from the coach to the player on all individual and team movements. The primary motive is to help the players develop the ability to play a faster, more dynamic game while maintaining good ball control skills.

SUMMARY AND GUIDELINES TO EFFECTIVE MOVEMENT TRAINING

1) Get out and observe experienced coaches train their teams to acquire more knowledge on drill development, physical conditioning and teaching keys.

2) Construct a program that is right for your institution or club. Purchase apparatus you know you can afford and will use regularly.

3) Create your own court movement circuits. Have your athletes perform movements (without using volleyballs) that closely resemble the movements required during the match.

4) Then, perform some movements (using volleyballs), first with resistance, then without. This form of "contrast" training will help the athlete get quicker by improving stride length and stride frequency. This is motor learning in its purest "kinesense." Use resistors or weight belts.

5) Use plyometrics regularly—vertical and lateral. Use short heights and quick steps. Build slowly. Eliminate depth jumping at lower levels. Start with squat thrusts, tuck jumps, cone jumps, square hops, straddle hops, push-ups and rope skipping. At higher levels, more height in jump training can be required.

6) Work at overspeed daily. Use high-knee motion, cone-to-cone acceleration runs, "fast-feet" exercises, resistor running, wind sprints, tag relays, board pushing, line drills, sprint circuits, hill running, etc.

7) Improve movement posture (i.e., keep the weight on the balls of the feet, pelvis rotated under, arms at right angles, lifting from the buttocks and hamstrings, not the extremities).

8) Combine speed and quickness building with flexibility work, ab-

According to Featherstone, a great way to learn effective movement training is to observe experienced coaches training their players.

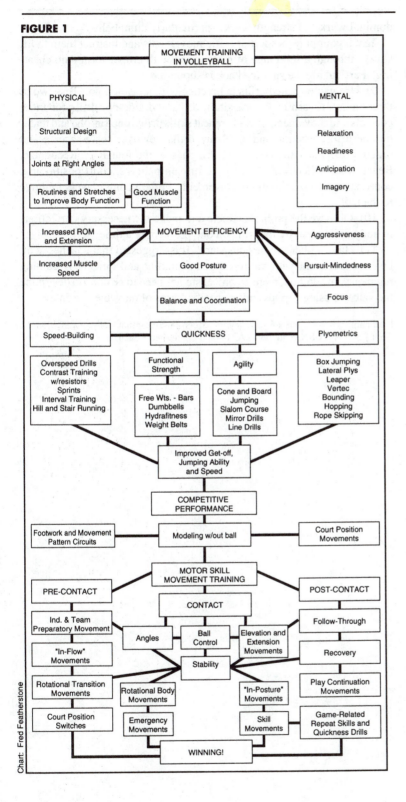

Movement training is not merely developing quickness and explosion. It involves constant feedback from the coach to the player on all individual and team movements. The primary motive is to help the players develop the ability to play a faster, more dynamic game while maintaining good ball control skills.

dominal work and strength work—particularly dumbbells.

Teach your players sport-specific movements and instruct them to lift slowly through a full range of motion and with proper form—no cheating. Particularly, be sure the back is supported.

9) Use game-related drills in practice with a fast tempo. Toss two to three balls in wash drills, transition drills and side-out drills for more contacts and movement. Include repeat skills drills, one-on-one and team-on-one drills, reaction and rapid-fire drills, revolver serve-receive and digging drills and stamina drills. Emphasize the four R's: Recognize, React, Reach, Recover. Emphasize linking patterns, court positioning, court balance and continuous movement. Force young players to move to the ball.

10) Observe the problem athlete and make the necessary corrections in body movement by focusing on one problem at a time.

11) Have a plan and be consistent. It is suggested that coaches at all levels experiment with various types of agility and quickness training regimens. In addition, more empirical studies need to be done to determine the value of using various and/or specific forms of movement training.

Fred Featherstone is the men's volleyball coach at Grossmont College (El Cajon, Calif.) and is a USA Volleyball CAP Level II accredited coach.

Section II: Dealing With Injury

Causes and Treatment of Muscle Cramps

Causes and Treatment of Muscle Cramps

In the fifth game of a match in a hot and stuffy gym, the setter goes up to set and comes down grimacing in pain, clutching her right calf. She has been sweating profusely throughout the match but has not been drinking much water at breaks. At the end of the play she is helped to the bench, where the trainer or assistant coach helps her work out an injury that often results from dehydration: muscle cramp.

Muscle cramps are painful, involuntary muscle contractions caused by dehydration, electrolyte imbalance or ischemia (an inadequate supply of blood to a muscle). Most often cramping occurs during exposure to severe hot or cold temperatures or as a result of overexercise, injury or irritation to the muscles.

The most familiar type of muscle cramp is a heat cramp, writes Bryant Stamford, Ph.D., in the February 1986 issue of *The Physician and Sportsmedicine*. Volleyball players can lose four to six pounds of water in an hour during long workouts or matches in a hot gym. Water is the best fluid replacement and should be consumed at the rate of 8 ounces per 20 minutes of activity, Stamford says.

Volleyball players can lose four to six pounds of water in an hour during long workouts or matches in a hot gym.

Heat cramps can also be caused by an electrolyte imbalance. Electrolytes such as potassium and sodium are responsible for generating the electrical activity involved in muscle contractions and for restoring the resting state, Stamford writes. Electrolytes are lost through sweat and as they are depleted, it becomes difficult for the muscles to return to the resting state.

Again, water replacement is the recommended treatment. Stamford also suggests the preventive treatment of eating foods high in electrolytes, such as bananas, oranges and fresh vegetables.

Volleyball players also risk ischemia; tight-fitting elastic (such as in knee pads) can cause loss of blood volume in a muscle. Injury to a muscle or joint can also cause cramping, Stamford writes, because the surrounding muscles contract to act as a natural splint to protect the injured area.

To relieve a cramp, forcefully stretch the muscle and the tendons that attach the muscle to the bone. This creates tension on the tendons and activates the endings that inhibit further muscle contractions.

CRAMP TREATMENT

To relieve a cramp, forcefully stretch the muscle and the tendons that attach the muscle to the bone, Stamford says. This creates tension on the tendons and activates the endings that inhibit further muscle contractions. This stretching technique is called reciprocal innervation: Every time you flex a muscle, the opposing muscle stretches to counterbalance it.

To relieve a calf muscle cramp, pull the toes and ball of the foot toward the kneecap. For a bicep cramp, flex the triceps while preventing movement at the elbow joint with the opposite hand. Stamford also suggests massaging the muscle once the cramp is relieved to increase blood flow to the muscle.

Cryotherapy is the use of cold for therapeutic treatment of injuries. It is the appropriate initial treatment for virtually all musculoskeletal injuries. Cryotherapy helps decrease pain and muscle spasms, produces numbness and decreases inflammation.

When there is an injury to the muscoskeletal system, the inflammatory process is initiated. Inflammation is the body's method of protecting and localizing the damaged area. It has primary and secondary phases.

With trauma, damage occurs to cells in the injured areas. The primary phase of inflammation involves cell death, hemorrhage (bleeding) and hematoma (pooling of blood). The secondary phase begins as damaged cells die and release enzymes called histamines. Histamines increase cappilary permeability, which allows fluid to leak through capillary walls. So, not only are damaged blood vessels leaking blood, but non-injured vessels leak plasma, proteins, colloids and water into the injured area. Both processes produce swelling or edema.

Signs of swelling/edema include: increased size when compared to uninjured body part; loss of normal color; increased tissue temperature at injury site; pain; redness; mucle splinting (spasm); and loss of function/restricted range of motion.

(Copyright 1993, United States Olympic Committee, Sports Medicine Division. Used with permission.)

NUTRITIONAL CONCERNS OF THE VEGETARIAN ATHLETE

Athletes on vegetarian or semivegetarian diets could run the risk of nutritional inadequacy, according to Ann Grandjean, former chief nutrition consultant for the U.S. Olympic Committee. Grandjean, in a May 1987 *Physician and Sportsmedicine* article, notes that as one's diet becomes more restrictive in food sources, it becomes more difficult to get all of the needed nutrients in sufficient amounts.

Grandjean says, however, that studies have shown that diets based on plant foods alone can be nutritionally adequate if they incorporate a source of vitamin B12, which is not found in plant sources. Other nutrients typically supplied in lower-than-recommended levels by vegetarian diets are protein, iron, riboflavin, calcium and zinc. Grandjean adds that athletes involved in vigorous training often require 3,000 to 6,000 calories daily. That level may be difficult to attain on a vegetarian diet, which typically focuses on foods high in bulk and low in calories (energy).

"Clearly, vegetarians can be successful world-class athletes," says Grandjean. "A good example is Chris Evert. But vegetarians need to make careful food selections to obtain adequate amounts of essential nutrients. Case in point: [collegiate and professional basketball player] Bill Walton followed a strict vegetarian diet for several years and many of his bone fracture problems were attributed to his diet."

WATER: THE CLASSIC FLUID FOR EXERCISE

Water is the most vital nutrient for those who exercise in the heat, says nutrition specialist Anne-Marie Davee, R.D. Dehydration occurs when fluid loss exceeds one percent of body weight. Athletes who are in excellent condition and are heat-acclimatized can perform until two to three percent of their body weight is lost in fluid.

Initial signs of dehydration include excessive thirst, chills, clammy skin, a throbbing heartbeat and nausea. To conserve what water is left, Davee writes, the body gradually stops sweating and internal temperatures rapidly rise. The blood becomes thicker and the heart pumps more furiously and less effectively.

Thirst is not an accurate barometer of your fluid needs, Davee writes. She suggests the following guidelines for hot weather exercisers:

• Drink eight glasses of water, fruit juice, milk, club soda or mineral water a day.

• Weigh yourself before and after training. For every pound of body weight that you have lost, drink 16 oz. of fluid.

• Drink fluids cold (40 to 45 degrees F) because they empty faster from the stomach.

• To avoid bloating, drink no more than 20 ounces at one time. Drink 20 ounces two hours and one hour before exercising; 8 to 10 ounces 15 minutes before exercising; and 4 to 10 ounces at 15-minute intervals during activity.

Athletes involved in vigorous training often require 3,000 to 6,000 calories daily. That level may be difficult to attain on a vegetarian diet, which typically focuses on foods high in bulk and low in calories (energy).

- Dilute sport drinks, fruit juices and sugar containing beverages because high sugar concentration slows absorption. (Five to eight percent sugar concentration is optimal.)

COLD MOST EFFECTIVE TO REDUCE SWELLING

Using cold therapy has long been the accepted method for treating sprained ankles, and the results of a recent study confirm the effectiveness of this procedure. Debra Cote and three others from the University of North Carolina at Chapel Hill tested the effectiveness of cold, heat and contrast baths in reducing edema (swelling) in sprained ankles. The results of the study, published in the July 1988 *Physical Therapy Journal*, showed that cold therapy was clearly the most effective method in reducing edema. Heat and contrast baths allowed almost identical increases in the amount of edema during all three days of the study.

Water replacement is the recommended treatment for muscle cramps caused by dehydration, which can occur easily in players who compete in a very hot gymnasium.

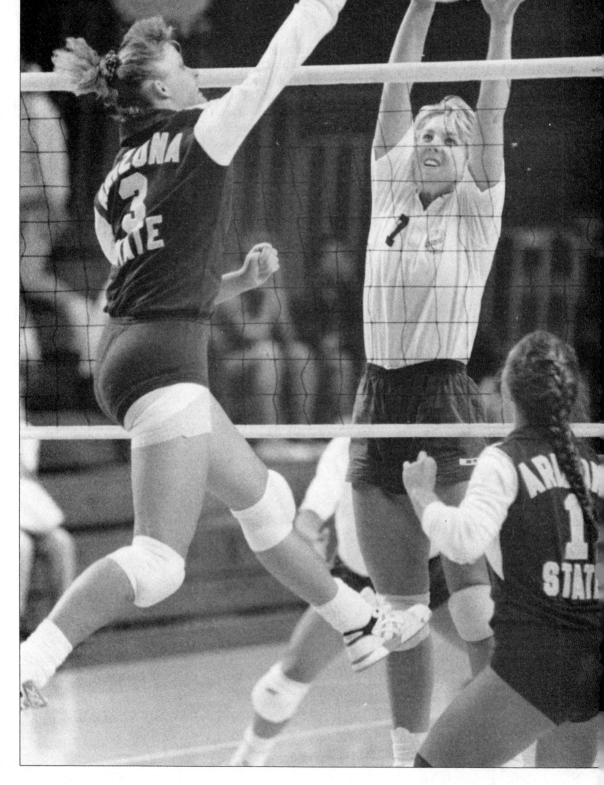

Psychological Ramifications for the Injured Athlete

Psychological Ramifications for the Injured Athlete

Cynthia Booth

This was the year Jayne thought would be hers. After struggling through difficult times her freshman and sophomore years, she earned a starting spot and was ready to take control. She led her team in both kills and hitting efficiency in the first two matches of the season, and she felt that, for the first time in three years, the roadblocks to her success were gone. Then, in her third match, she landed on another player's foot and severely sprained her ankle. After the match Jayne's coach asked the trainer how long it would take Jayne to return. "Physically, maybe three or four weeks," answered the trainer. "Her emotional recovery, however, poses an entirely different question."

If injured athletes receive rehabilitation that addresses both the physical aspects and psychological concerns, they will be more confident in returning to participation.

The goal of any rehabilitation program is to return the athlete to the competitive level prior to injury. Therapeutic modalities assist athletic trainers in the physical treatment and rehabilitation of injuries, but attention also needs to be directed toward the psychological status of injured athletes. A coach must work carefully with the athletic trainer to explore fully the psychological ramifications of an injury and must take the steps necessary to ensure the athlete's full recovery, both physically and emotionally.

It is often assumed that athletes who attain a prescribed level of physical rehabilitation are ready to return safely to participation. However, this is not true for all athletes. Some adapt psychologically to injury more readily than others. We see the same phenomenon in physical rehabilitation. If injured athletes receive rehabilitation that addresses both the physical aspects and psychological concerns, they will be more confident in returning to participation. Of course, there will always be some athletes who will just not feel ready to compete no matter what assurances we give them. According to Rotella and Heyman (1986), a premature return to competition may lead to one or more of the following:

- reinjury;
- injury to another body part;
- lowered confidence, resulting in a temporary or permanent performance loss; and/or
- generalized depression and fear of further injury, which can sap motivation and the desire to compete.

> Research with athletes suggests that certain psychological factors may predispose some individuals to injury and reinjury. Identifying those predisposing factors enables us to watch for problems among athletes who may be at risk.

Athletic trainers are concerned with preventing athletic injuries. Research with athletes suggests that certain psychological factors may predispose some individuals to injury and reinjury. Identifying those predisposing factors enables us to watch for problems among athletes who may be at risk. Rotella and Heyman further emphasize that stressful life events, such as the death of a family member, a move, or trouble in academic or athletic performance have been cited as factors affecting predisposition to injury. Anxiety created by such events, in turn, creates muscular tension. Attentional focus narrows (concentration is decreased) and injury may occur as a result of tensed muscles. Control of anxiety and muscular tension must thus be

...ch phase of the injury and rehabilitation process yields emotional reactions. The patient's experiences will vary depending on the degree of disability, the type of therapeutic interventions pursued and the success of said intervention. It must be emphasized that each aspect of rehabilitation brings with it a variety of emotional responses from the patient. The range is from anxiety and fear to newfound confidence; from sadness, anger and frustration to elation and satisfaction. It is the challnege of the therapist to gauge the patient's emotional state, as well as assess the physical well-being while guiding and facilitating the rehabilitation.

(Depper PhD., Devora and Richard Ritter. The psychology of rehabilitation. *Coaching Volleyball*, August/September 1991, 25.)

considered in injury prevention. Paper-and-pencil tests can be used with players to identify the types and amounts of stress in their lives and may help red-flag athletes susceptible to injury.

Many coaches teach that mental toughness and giving more than 100 percent all the time are necessary for success in sport. This is partly true, but athletes also need to know that when taken to extremes, this philosophy can lead to injury or failure. Some coaches reward players for "playing tough" or playing with pain; "no pain no gain" echoes through their practices. Instead, we need to teach athletes which pains to listen to and which to ignore.

In time, athletes who continually give that 110 percent develop a false image of invulnerability. Then when they get hurt, they cannot cope–they are totally unprepared for their injuries. One football player stated in an interview, "I never imagined ever being hurt. I give my all every time I am out on the field. I have never missed a practice; I have never sat out. Coach always told me that I would go far with the drive and dedication I have. He told me that I had guts and that I played harder than anyone he had ever seen. I always gave more than 100 percent. I cannot sit out now—it is only a knee sprain."

The mental games played by some coaches can damage athletes both physically and psychologically. Some coaches tend to alienate injured athletes, to consider them worthless. Another player explained, "Coach does not even care. He came in the day I got hurt and said suck it up and go. Then when I showed I could not, he treated me as if I were not even on the team."

Some coaches think that making injured athletes feel unimportant will speed their recovery, that they can hurry and get well. Others identify injured players by having them wear different colored jerseys or remain in a separated group. Identity becomes an embarrassment and other players begin to treat the injured ones differently, as well. Some may make injured athletes feel guilty that they are not helping the team win. Others suggest that they are not mentally tough and that "you have to take some pain."

Psychological rehabilitation in response to physical injury, then, should be a concern of every athletic trainer and coach. We should treat not only the injury but the individual, as well. Understanding the athlete's psychological response to injury will enhance rehabilitation. Rehabilitation programs should be tailored to the needs of individual athletes.

Lidstone (1988) identified these psychological consequences of an athletic injury:
- Pain
- Grief
- Frustration
- Anger
- Disability
- Alienation
- Fear

- Decreased sense of self-worth
- Being forced to seek alternatives.

Athletes vary in the ability and desire to cope with pain. Although the pain experienced by every player is real, the degree depends on the individual. Inherent in any irreversible loss is grief. Elizabeth Kubler-Ross, in her classic book *On Death and Dying* (1969), identified a five-stage grief response of (1) denial, disbelief and isolation; (2) anger; (3) bargaining; (4) depression; and (5) acceptance.

Such stages of adjustment to loss can be seen among athletes who suffer injuries. Often injured athletes are initially in a shock-like state. They might react by saying, "There is no damage," or "The injury is not that bad," or "I will be back ready tomorrow." But when tomorrow comes and the injury remains, they become frustrated and angry. Anger may be directed at trainers, coaches, teammates or family members. It may be vented verbally or acted out in breaking training or team rules.

Anger is followed by a true sense of loss. It is common for injured athletes to focus on the seriousness of their injuries: "Is the disability short-term or long-term? Is it the end of my career?" As athletes realize the extent of their disabilities, they tend to isolate themselves from the other players. The unique bond among athletes on a team sometimes breaks when a player is injured. The athlete no longer feels part of the team and may be ostracized by the coaches and players. Comments like "Hurry and get well soon; you are missing a lot; we could really use you" cause the athlete to withdraw further.

> As athletes realize the extent of their disabilities, they tend to isolate themselves from the other players. The unique bond among athletes on a team sometimes breaks when a player is injured. The athlete no longer feels part of the team and may be ostracized by the coaches and players.

Fears and anxieties often accompany injury. Lidstone (1988) described the fears of injured athletes:
- reinjury on return to competition;
- not recovering;
- losing a position;
- losing a job (profession); and/or
- losing a scholarship.

Injury is traumatic for athletes. It can cause extreme anxiety in which they lose appetite, sleep and self-esteem. A female basketball player shared that "my biggest fear is landing on another person's foot when coming down from a rebound. Often I visualize stepping on someone's foot and feeling my ankle crack."

Also associated with injury is a decreased sense of self-worth. Injured athletes may feel they can no longer contribute to or are no longer valued members of the team.

Finally, injured athletes are forced to seek alternatives to their previous levels of play. They have to make small to drastic modifications in activity, depending on the severity of their injuries. They might play different positions, not go after the ball as aggressively or quit completely.

The response of athletes to injury has also been described by Wiese and Weiss (1987) and Weiss and Troxel (1986) as one of stress and grief. They propose that athletes pass through four stages of stress response to injury.

The stress response begins with the question "What happened?" The injury is the stressor, placing considerable demand and constraint on the body to adapt. Second, the athlete begins to appraise the injury cognitively. What does the athlete think about what happened? Is it threatening or nonthreatening, pleasant or unpleasant? What is the extent of damage? Injured athletes may feel they have let their coaches or teammates down. Negative self-talk patterns may begin: "What if I do not come back? What will the coach think of me?" These factors impact the third stage—emotional response. Physiological arousal occurs as blood pressure and pulse change. Anxiety and worry may develop, which can increase muscle tension and the cycle continues.

Finally comes the behavioral consequence of the physical and psychological responses: What will the athlete do about what happened? Athletes' behaviors determine whether they recover successfully from injury. And, of course, coaches had athletes who do recover "in spite of us."

The Wiese, Weiss, and Troxel model allows for a better understanding of the psychological reaction of the athlete to injury. We must realize, however, that an athlete's behavior may vary throughout the course of an injury as a result of the interaction of personal attributes and situational factors. Personal attributes include anxiety, self-concept and motivation. Situational factors include the timing of an injury, the type of sport and pressure from coaches, team or parents. An injury during preseason may not be as psychologically significant as one in the middle of the season.

According to Booth, an injury during preseason may not be as psychologically significant as one in the middle of the season.

The overall implication of all of this information is that athletic trainers and coaches must realize that each individual is different. They must modify rehabilitation programs to fit individual physical and psychological needs to achieve the goal of rehabilitation: to return the injured athlete to the pre-injury competitive level.

There are many ways to help athletes cope with injury. Physical agents such as medications, modalities, surgery and therapy are traditional in rehabilitation. But how in tune are we psychologically? Many psychological strategies can complement the physical rehabilitation process. Knowing athletes as individuals provides the foundation for communication. Learning background information—the athlete's previous injury history or role on the team—is important in evaluating an injury, as is ascertaining motivational level, self-talk patterns and reaction to the stress of injury. The coach and athletic trainer should work cooperatively in gathering this information from the injured athlete.

I feel that the most important rehabilitative intervention is communication. The athletic trainer should clearly explain the injury to the athlete, in as much detail as possible. The nature of the injury and what to expect with regard to pain, activity limitations and the length of rehabilitation should be outlined in language that the athlete can understand. The athletic trainer should give the rationale for every treatment so the athlete can understand the "whys" of it all. Understanding why he or she is doing a certain treatment or exercise helps the athlete develop trust and control, alleviates fears and promotes better rapport with the trainer.

Weiss and Troxel (1986) stated that injured athletes tend to dwell on irrational or negative thoughts. "What if?" statements are prevalent. "What if I get behind in training?" "What if I do not get back in time to finish the season?" "What if I get reinjured?" These thought patterns perpetuate the stress response to injury.

The athlete needs to be guided toward positive and task-related thoughts. This can be achieved as the athletic trainer, the coach and the injured athlete work together to establish realistic and attainable rehabilitation goals. The athlete needs to realize that positive self-talk will enhance performance in rehabilitation. Thoughts produce actions—if positive thinking is present, the actions will be rewarding.

Another means by which the athletic trainer can help the athlete's rehabilitation is setting short-term and long-term goals, written so that the athlete can see progression. The goals should be challenging, motivating, and realistic. The coach can also assist in the rehabilitation program; once the injured athlete can begin exercising outside the training room, the coach, the athlete and the athletic trainer should outline a plan incorporating sport-specific exercises.

Progressive goals boost the athlete's confidence and motivation. Goals should be evaluated frequently and rewritten as rehabilitation progresses. Goal attainment should be easy if goals are measurable and observable (e.g., "By Monday, lift five pounds on the SLR" or "Increase range of motion by five degrees in flexion and extension by Friday"). Goals can help motivate injured athletes to persist in putting forth effort for recovery.

Physical accomplishments in rehabilitation can bring a sense of psychological accomplishment as well. Further emotional support for injured athletes can come in the form of modeling and injury support groups.

In peer modeling, an injured athlete is linked with players who have successfully recovered from similar injuries. These individuals provide support and encouragement and serve as positive models for the injured athlete. In an injury support group, injured athletes meet regularly with the athletic trainer, the coach, and/or a sport psychologist to discuss their thoughts and emotions. The injured athletes learn that they are not alone in suffering injuries and they are helped to readjust and cope with life change in an attempt to decrease their injury vulnerability.

Another useful psychological strategy is relaxation. Relaxation exercises can be taught to the injured athlete (preferably by a sport psychologist—the athletic trainer or coach should seek advice from a counseling center or local psychologist). The exercises serve to calm the athlete and help shift attention away from worry and tension to more positive thoughts.

> Another means by which the athletic trainer can help the athlete's rehabilitation is setting short-term and long-term goals, written so that the athlete can see progression. The goals should be challenging, motivating and realistic. The coach can also assist in the rehabilitation program; once the injured athlete can begin exercising outside the training room, the coach, the athlete and the athletic trainer should outline a plan incorporating sport-specific exercises.

Mental imagery is a final psychological intervention that can influence an athlete's response to injury. In imaging, athletes learn to control their visual images and to direct them productively to reduce tension.

An ideal situation would be to have a sport psychologist on staff to enhance the "psychological" knowledge of the coach, athletic trainer and athlete in dealing with the injury cycle.

SUMMARY

Research, interviews with athletes and personal experience all testify to the importance of utilizing psychological skills in injury management. Athletic trainers and coaches who understand the psychological responses that athletes encounter when they face the stress of injury can aid in their rehabilitation. Communication skills—being an effective listener, being positive, giving feedback and being honest—are critical to establishing good rapport with an injured athlete. We must learn to treat the person, not just the injury.

Remember, athletes are human beings—treat them as individuals. Understanding the definite relationship between the physical and psychological aspects of rehabilitation and implementing both in the rehabilitation process creates an optimal healing environment.

REFERENCES

Arnheim, D. (1985). *Modern Principles of Athletic Training*. Los Angeles: Times Mirror Publishers.

Kubler-Ross, E. *On Death and Dying*. London: MacMillan.

Lamb, M. (1986). Self-concept and injury frequency among female college field hockey players. *Athletic Training, 21*, 220-224.

Lidstone, J. (1988). Psychology of athletic rehabilitation. Presentation at the NAIA District 5 Convention.

Pargman, D. (1987). Helping and understanding the injured athlete: implications for the sports medicine team. *The Sport Psychologist, 1*, 318-330.

Pargman, D. (1987). Psychological aspects of sport injury. Florida *Journal of Health, Physical Education, Recreation and Dance*, 25(3), 43-45.

Pederson, P. (1986). The grief response and injury: a special challenge for athletes and athletic trainers. *Athletic Training, 21(4)*, 312-314.

Rotella, R.J., and Heymann, S. (1986). Stress injury and the psychological rehabilitation of athletes. *Applied Sport Psychology*. Palo Alto, CA: Mayfield.

Singer, R.N. and P.J. Johnson. (1987). Strategies to cope with pain associated with sport-related injuries. *Athletic Training, 22(2)*, 100-103.

Wiese, D.M. and M.R. Weiss. (1987). Psychological rehabilitation and physical injury: implications for the sports medicine team. *The Sport Psychologist, 1*, 318-330.

Weiss, M.R. and R.K. Troxel. (1986). Psychology of the injured athlete. *Athletic Training, 21(2)*, 104-105, 154.

Cynthia Booth, MS, ATC, is an instructor in the Health and Physical Education Department at Moorhead State University (Moorhead, Minn.).

Section III: Psychology of Sport

The Psychology of Optimal Volleyball:
Teaching Mental Skills to Physical People

The Psychology of Optimal Volleyball: Teaching Mental Skills to Physical People

NATE ZINSSER, PH.D., AND
ROBERT GAMBARDELLA

The notion that the mind has a powerful effect on sport performance is hardly new. Ancient cultures in Greece and Asia acknowledged the interdependence of mind and body for both personal development and maximum effectiveness. In North America, books documenting the impact of the mind on sport performance began appearing in 1908 and have increased in number and complexity since then. The television and other news media frequently focus on the concentration, poise and confidence required to perform at high levels (e.g., the coverage devoted to the collapse of Olympic decathlon hopeful Dan O'Brien in July/August 1992 and speedskater Dan Jansen in 1994).

Despite this interest, many coaches have not had the opportunity to develop the intuitive understanding of the mental skills affecting performance to the point where it can be effectively communicated to their athletes. The chapters in this section will begin to address this situation by providing coaches with some of the basic information on mental skills training and how it can be facilitated. The emphasis will be on information which can be immediately conveyed to athletes to help them become more aware of how they can use their minds to reach optimal performance levels. While not a substitute for in-depth study of applied sport psychology, these readings will provide a conceptual framework and hopefully whet the appetite for further exploration.

This chapter addresses the question: 1) "How can coaches best introduce and create interest in mental skills training?" This question will be answered in two sections. First, some background on sport psychology will be provided, designed to demystify the concept of mental skills training. The points developed in this section are appropriate for opening up discussion on mental training and putting to rest the athletes' fear of "psychology." The second section offers the coach a series of questions and examples which are useful in communicating to athletes the logic and necessity of exploring one's attitude and developing more effective mental skills.

This chapter will conclude with a summary and a description of certain key mental skills, each of which will be the subject of a separate chapter in this section.

Coaches can become familiar with information which can be immediately conveyed to athletes to help them become more aware of how they can use their minds to reach optimal performance levels.

It is important to use the word psychology very cautiously when talking to athletes since many of them (and many coaches, as well) share the common perception that psychology is a mysterious, inexact science focused primarily on the treatment of mental illness.

WHAT IS SPORT PSYCHOLOGY?

It is important to use the word psychology very cautiously when talking to athletes since many of them (and many coaches, as well) share the common perception that psychology is a mysterious inexact science focused primarily on the treatment of mental illness. Delving into this con-

To help athletes reach optimal success, ask them to re-experience their best performances mentally in practice and in games.

An important variable associated with the achievement motivation process is coaching behavior. How a coach develops and maintains individual and team achievement motivation must be closely examined.

Coaches are often so intensely involved in teaching correct athletic skills–the content–that they are unaware of their methodology, or the process. Coaches must use consistent and appropriate positive and negative reinforcement (extrinsic motivation) with their athletes. Common positive reinforcement (rewards) includes verbal praise, attendance on away trips, starting during a match or a varsity letter.

Negative reinforcement might include exclusion from an unpopular conditioning drill or from carrying equipment on an away trip. Negative reinforcement encourages player performance behavior by allowing players to avoid aversive situations.

When a new skill is taught, it should be broken down into components and players should be rewarded for successfully performing each one until the complete skill is properly performed. The bottom line is to execute volleyball skills properly, with rewards coming from both intrinsic (players providing their own self-rewards) and extrinsic levels.

(LeBoeuf, Joseph and Robert Gambardella. Achieving volleyball excellence through sport psychology. *Coaching Volleyball*, December/January 1988, 7-8.)

fusing and often contradictory world seems irrelevant to the pursuit of excellence in sport. For this reason, sport psychology can be carried on under the label "performance enhancement" a term which conveys only positive outcomes. Such a re-wording is highly recommended (other possibilities are "effectiveness training" or "achievement instruction") as the last thing most athletes want is some "psychologist" or "shrink" analyzing their dreams or probing them with questions about their early childhood.

Any discussion of psychology as it applies to athletics should begin with the explanation that the psychology of enhanced performance and "psychology" as it is commonly perceived are two totally different fields of study with totally different purposes. While "psychology" evolved from medicine and follows the medical model's assumption that the patient (i.e., the athlete) is sick or unhealthy or abnormal and thus in need of help in order to become "normal," the psychology of enhanced performance assumes that athletes are in general very healthy to begin with and may benefit from some fine tuning of the mental skills they were born with in order to become excellent or supernormal performers.

As a way of expressing this we have found it useful in an introductory session to state to a group of athletes that the last thing we want is for anyone on our teams to be "normal" because high-level sport performance has nothing to do with being "normal." Instead, we encourage athletes to think of themselves as very different from anyone else. We want to be different, even to the point of being abnormal as these are just other ways of saying that we want to be great! Because we want to stand out and be the best, the theory, the data and the methods employed by modern psychology over the years to help sick people become normal is useless to us as athletes and top performers. By stressing this difference of purpose coaches can help their athletes set aside their associations with the word "psychology" and realize that white lab coats discussions of mental illness and dream analysis do not apply to performance enhancement.

To help athletes understand this distinction clearly, offer them a functional and positive definition of sport psychology. Instead of describing sport psychology as the application of psychological techniques to sport and athletic training, refer to it as the study of how attitudes, beliefs and thinking habits affect physical performance. This definition will remove the mystery and stigma commonly associated with psychology and replace it with a positive understanding that thoughts and beliefs have an impact on volleyball performance.

To help athletes understand this in more personal terms, ask them to re-experience their best performances ("Go back to the best match you ever played...see what you saw during that match...hear what you heard...feel what you felt during that match..."). Ask the athletes to recall the thoughts and feelings they were having during these moments of great performance and write a sentence or a paragraph describing their state of mind, the way they talked to themselves, their level of concentration. Repeat this process, recalling a particularly poor performance and compare the two descriptions. Athletes will readily see that their thoughts and feelings during high-level performances have a very different quality than those experienced during poor performances. If offered the choice, which of these two thought/feeling states would they find more useful? Mental training is simply the process of becoming more aware of this desired mental state and taking the necessary steps to ensure that one can enter it at will.

Some further points are important to emphasize at this time. Applied sport psychology is not magic; it does not guarantee success at all times. Like strength training or proper nutrition, it increases the odds in one's favor and gives one a greater chance of success by controlling an unknown variable. Neither is mental training a quick fix which can be done once early in the season and then abandoned. Developing confidence, improving one's ability to focus under pressure and keeping one's attention in the present are all skills which evolve with practice and commitment. Just as practice time is routinely scheduled for quickness drills or for stretching, time must also be regularly allotted for players to practice relaxation, concentration and other mental skills. Finally, sport psychology is not a last resort for those players or teams who have tried "everything else" in order to succeed. It is, instead, one component of an athlete's overall development; although new at this time, it must become a regular part of training just as technical skill, cardiovascular conditioning and muscular strength already are. Despite the fact that the mental preparation of athletes has been approached somewhat haphazardly in the past, coaches can help athletes take greater responsibility for their success in volleyball by providing encouragement and guidance to the athlete who really wishes to find out how well they can play.

WHY BOTHER WITH "MENTAL TRAINING?"

Athletes generally accept the notion that they will have to work systematically to improve their technique, their strength and their other physical capacities (endurance, flexibility, etc.). The notion of systematically working on their attitude (on the quality of their thinking) is far less commonly accepted, but crucial to their ultimate success as players or as team members. To impress upon players the importance of developing a great attitude, the following ideas, suitable as an agenda for a team meeting, are presented.

First, ask the athletes to consider the realty of the world of their sport today. With so many teams putting in more hours of training, using the latest developments in exercise physiology (plyometrics, PNF stretching) and video technology, success in volleyball has become a greater challenge than ever. Given that most teams are doing all they can to maximize their physical training, what will determine the outcome when two teams which are evenly matched physically face each other? The answer is simply attitude. The winner is going to be the team that believes in itself at the moment of truth, the team that can best throw away any and all fear and the team that can handle any and all distractions and

A team huddle following an opponent's side-out allows players to deal collectively– and then individually– with anxiety, tension, confusion and attentional focus. Most rallies end with a negative play. Between plays, many athletes and teams fail to deal positively with psychological factors. The player responsible for the error often displays negative body language (hanging the head, muttering to him/herself, wandering around the court not knowing the next serve reception position).

Huddling before the next play ensures that the athlete is not isolated from the team (lessens anxious feelings); it provides close contact with teammates (relieves tension); it identifies sequential response (avoids confusion); and it assists in calling the next play sets (focuses attention). After the huddle the athlete can deal individually with remaining negative psychological factors.

In practice, athletes should develop not only physical skills, but also mental ones for controlling negative psychological factors. The method you teach should be inclusive, yet simple enough to perform in a few seconds during game conditions. Athletes can cognitively practice a variety of techiques in drills, first independently and then collectively, to improve their performance.

(Cox, Richard H. and Jerre L. McManama. The psychological side of women's volleyball. *Coaching Volleyball*, August/September 1988, 22.)

simply play the game one point at a time. Once athletes acknowledge this fact of sport, they will begin to understand the necessity of developing a winning attitude.

To drive home this point further, ask your athletes to list on one side of a sheet of paper the physical skills and attributes they will need to develop and consistently demonstrate in order to succeed. In no time at all, an impressive list of general physical skills and specific volleyball skills will be generated. Next, ask the athletes to generate a list of mental skills necessary for success on the other side of their paper. Simple responses such as confidence, concentration, intensity and motivation are perfectly acceptable. Now ask for a show of hands in response to the questions, "How much of your success as a player is determined by these mental skills? How many of you feel that mental skills account for at least 10 percent of your success? How many feel these skills account for 25 percent of your success? 50 percent? 60 percent? 75 percent? 80 percent?" Typically, everyone on a team will concur that mental skills comprise 10-25 percent of their success, while usually half the team will agree that 50 percent of success comes from these factors. Some team members, typically a fourth of any given team, will confidently state that mental factors account for the large majority of their success. Next, ask the athletes how many hours they typically spend each week over the course of the season developing and perfecting the physical skills they identified previously and how many hours they spend developing their mental skills. Finally, ask each player to consider honestly if the time they devote to these two areas accurately reflects the importance they just assigned to them. Almost without exception, athletes will discover that while they admit that mental skills such as concentration, confidence and patience are responsible for a significant portion of their success, they devote very little time to building these skills systematically.

This simple exercise in self-awareness can lead to the realization that important determinants of volleyball success are being neglected. No player would ignore developing quickness or endurance, but many players might be tempted to leave the development of their concentration or relaxation skills to chance, despite having just recognized these very same skills as essential to their overall success. Is this in their own best interest?

> Almost without exception, athletes will discover that while they admit that mental skills such as concentration, confidence and patience are responsible for a significant portion of their success, they devote very little time to building these skills systematically.

Asking these questions will help the athlete come to an important personal decision about moving forward and developing their potential versus neglecting their mental side of performance out of ignorance or out of habit.

SUMMARY

A rationale for devoting time and energy to training the mind has been provided, urging athletes to look honestly at the determinants of their success. The questions and concepts presented in this chapter can become the outline for a team meeting ideally suited to the outset of a new season, but are worth introducing at any point. Future chapters in this section will focus on key mental skills (effective thinking, attention control, relaxation arousal, goal setting, visualization), their importance in volleyball and how they can be developed both individually and with the team.

RECOMMENDED INTRODUCTORY READINGS

Gallwey, Tim. (1974). *The Inner Game of Tennis.* New York: Random House.

Williams, Jean, ed. (1992). *Applied Sport Psychology: Personal Growth to Peak Performance*, Second Edition, Mountain View, CA: Mayfield Publishing.

Millman, Dan. (1979). *The Warrior Athlete*. Stillpoint Publishing.

Application Questions

1. How would you best explain to your athletes the differences between mental training for enhanced volleyball performance and "psychology" as it is commonly understood?

2. What do you think are the key mental skills which are important to success in volleyball? What portion of your team's success do high levels of these skills account for? What anecdotes could you provide from your coaching experience about the impact of mental training and high levels of mental readiness on individual and team volleyball success?

3. What are the costs and benefits to your program of 10 minutes of practice time each day devoted to mental training?

Nate Zinsser, Ph.D., is a sport psychologist at the United States Military Academy's Center for Enhanced Performance. Robert Gambardella is the former head women's volleyball coach at the U.S. Military Academy, the current director of youth development and programs for USA Volleyball and a CAP Level III accredited coach.

The Psychology of Optimal Volleyball: Effective Thinking

The Psychology of Optimal Volleyball: Effective Thinking

NATE ZINSSER, PH.D. AND
ROBERT GAMBARDELLA

As Martin Seligman, a psychologist at the University of Pennsylvania, writes in his book *Learned Optimism*, "Pessimists may have a better grasp of reality, but optimists live longer, perform better and have more fun."

The face and voice of Muhammed Ali are familiar to millions of Americans and millions of other sports fans around the world. For better than a decade, he was the best known sports figure, if not the most widely recognized person on the planet, known as much for his powerful personality as for his boxing achievements. Despite the fact that he barely graduated from high school, Ali knew the first and most important mental skill for the athlete, for the performer, for anyone who truly desires to succeed. That is the skill of effective thinking–using the mind's power of selective attention in a way that maximizes one's chances of success. He knew intuitively that eventually you become what you think you are.

Philosophers, scientists and poets have known for thousands of years that our attitudes, beliefs and thinking habits define the way we see the world, the way we feel inside and the way we behave. The Roman emperor Marcus Aurelius understood this when he wrote "Your life is what your thoughts make it." Walt Whitman, the great American writer, understood this when he wrote "A man is what he thinks about, all day long." And William James, the father of American psychology, when asked what he considered to be the most important scientific finding of the 19th century, replied, "The greatest discovery of my generation is that people can alter their lives by altering their habits of mind."

Despite this long and well-documented history, the idea of "positive" thinking is still today often greeted with sarcasm. To think "positively" conjures up visions of starry-eyed dreamers or young children who are ignorant of the world's true nature and who have not yet learned how to be "realistic." But if we regard positive thinking as an anomaly, are we not implicitly stating that it is "normal" to think negatively — that is, to expect the worse, to continually doubt oneself, to have low expectations so that we will not be let down? The question is not which of these thinking styles is the more correct, but which offers athletes and other performers the best chances of success. As Martin Seligman, a psychologist at the University of Pennsylvania writes in his book *Learned Optimism*, "Pessimists may have a better grasp of reality, but optimists live longer, perform better and have more fun."

Because of the unfortunate stigma associated with "positive" thinking, the term "effective" thinking is recommended when working with athletes. Effective thinking is a key attribute of successful athletes, based on the simple truths that the body follows the mind, that conscious thoughts lead directly to how one feels physically and emotionally and that these feelings in turn lead directly to athletic performance.

> Despite [a] long and well-documented history, the idea of "positive" thinking is still today often greeted with sarcasm. To think "positively" conjures up visions of starry-eyed dreamers or young children who are ignorant of the world's true nature and who have not yet learned how to be "realistic."

Many athletes are hesitant to explore the connection between how they think and how they perform. This could be because their thoughts seem to occur spontaneously and involuntarily and thus appear to be beyond their conscious control. But with a little knowledge and a little practice in the skills of effective thinking, any athlete can discipline his or her thought processes and use them to facilitate learning and performance. Any athlete can learn to replace critical, negative, self-defeating thoughts and statements with positive ones, learn to reinterpret events in ways that energize and excite him/her, and learn to focus the mind on those aspects of the environment that support continued effort and practice. By doing so, the athlete initiates the self-fulfilling prophecies that produce the actions to bring about success.

THE BASIS OF EFFECTIVE THINKING

There are three skills which form the basis of effective thinking: selective perception, controlling self-talk and using affirmations.

Selective Perception

Selective perception is a term for describing how one views oneself, one's environment and the events that take place in that environment. A volleyball player who has mastered this skill has a growth-oriented view of life, which allows him/her to perceive events in a positive and self-enhancing way. Regardless of what actually happens to the athlete, reality is perceived through a kind of personal mental filter.

This filter only allows successful confidence enhancing experiences to pass through and remain in the player's long-term memory. Memories of poor performances, failures and disappointments are caught in the filter and not allowed into the long-term memory. Sometimes these memories are altered as they pass through this filter, so that confidence can be gained even from these, stopping fear and self-doubt from taking hold. By using this filter, which we all have (and which we all can cultivate), a player can perform poorly nine times out of 10 and only recall the one success; miss three straight blocks and know that he/she will make the next one; hit four serves long and know that the next one will be on target.

Every player needs to evaluate honestly the personal tendency for interpreting events. The key question to ask and encourage is: "Do I think more about my best assets, my past good performances and my bright future or more about my liabilities my past poor performances, and the possibility that I will play poorly in the future?" The answer one finds to this question is the clearest indicator of whether one is thinking effectively or ineffectively.

Unfortunately, there are many athletes who seem to have a natural tendency or have somehow learned to perceive events in a self-defeating manner. They see themselves as victims of others or of their circumstances and when a change in their thinking habits is suggested they respond: "This is just the way I am," or "I have always been this way." Thus, they remain obedient to a self-defeating form of perception, a perception which allows them to perform well nine out of 10 times but only remember the one failure. Again, it is critical to evaluate honestly one's tendency and take control of these perceptions because they are at work all the time. If left to operate unchecked, they can condition an athlete to respond and react to a situation in ways that might not be in his or her best

By using a personal mental filter, which we all have (and which we all can cultivate), a player can perform poorly nine times out of 10 and only recall the one success.

Sport is the type of environment replete with evaluative experiences. Given the evaluative nature of self-acceptance, self-accepting athletes may experience less competitive cognitive anxiety than non self-accepting athletes. They have a sense of inherent self-worth just because they are human and exist (Branden 1983). Given the security that accompanies maintaining their self-worth and value as a human being, self-accepting athletes may experience less anxiety, more trust and confidence and less fear of failure than less self-accepting athletes. As a result, they may also send to perform better.

The "self" investment (self-worth involvement) an athlete makes with performance indirectly relates to performance by directly relating to cognitive anxiety.

(Hurley, Erin and Brett Mills. Examining self-acceptance: a new approach to performance. *Coaching Volleyball*, June/July 1993, 22.)

interest.

If athletes tend to hang onto memories of failures rather than memories of success; if they do not honestly see themselves as ready, willing and able to handle anything and beat anyone they might face; and if they still really want to give themselves the best chance to succeed, then they must decide to acquire and consciously practice this mindset, this selective perception. Doing so is as simple as looking in a mirror. Encourage players to focus on and appreciate their best features each time they pass that mirror, instead of immediately picking out the flaws and focusing on imperfections. Have players generate lists of their best assets and abilities as an athlete (endurance, hand-eye coordination, specific skills, etc.), and lists of their accomplishments (both in and out of sports), as ways of learning to focus on their own positive aspects.

> ...athletes must be encouraged to face higher ranked or very successful opponents with the attitude, "I am better than he/she until they prove otherwise," and take the time to find something positive and helpful to focus on in every practice, every drill and every player, rather than get caught up in anger and blame when frustrated by events beyond their control.

In the same vein, athletes must be encouraged to face higher ranked or very successful opponents with the attitude, "I am better than he/she until they prove otherwise," and take the time to find something positive and helpful to focus on in every practice, every drill and every play, rather than get caught up in anger and blame when frustrated by events beyond their control. In each of these situations it is easy to see that one course of thinking leaves the player feeling optimistic and energized while the other course leaves one demoralized and psychologically disadvantaged. The critical question is which choice gives you the best chance of success in this competitive world? The bottom line is that if a player wants to make it that players must decide to perceive in themselves and their environment those things which are going to allow and help them to get where they want to be.

Controlling Self-Talk

The next skill to consider in our discussion of effective thinking is with a habit everyone has: self-talk. It is a natural human activity to engage in some kind of internal dialogue and people get used to a little voice that chatters away in the back of their mind.

Much of the time we are not aware of this voice, much less aware of its specific content. However, if players are to perform at their best, they must become aware of, and then achieve control over this internal dialogue because these thoughts directly affect the way they feel and thus their chances of future success.

It is important to ask players to evaluate honestly the quality of their self-talk. What would they find if they did? Would it be generally positive — do they talk to themselves about what they want to happen? Or would it be generally negative; are they focused on what they do not want, or are afraid of? Does the quality of this self-talk change as they go from practice to match play? Before crucial points? When playing a team that is undefeated? Just as important, are these players able to catch themselves thinking ineffectively, immediately stop that train of thought

It has been observed that a 50 percent expectancy for success elicits the highest measurement for achievement motivation. This is what is known as risk-taking behavior. Risk-taking behavior is an extension of Atkinson's Theory of Achievement Motivation. Athletes high in achievement motivation seek out competitive situations in which there is a 50 percent chance of failure and avoid competitive situations in which the opponent is below their own ability.

(Mills, Brett. Achievement motivation: a practical application to volleyball. *Coaching Volleyball*, April/May 1993, 22.)

According to the authors, because athletes are only able to do what they think they can do, a strong belief in him or herself allows the freedom to use his or her full talents.

Perhaps the classic example of the power of affirmation to affect sport performance is Muhammed Ali's "I am the greatest."

and deliberately talk to themselves about what they want?

Fortunately, athletes are presented with numerous opportunities to practice this control every day. It is a sure bet that five times today everyone reading this article will engage in an ineffective inner dialogue, entertaining a fear about the future, criticizing oneself long after the moment has passed, or simply drifting into a conversation about something irrelevant to the situation at hand. Did you catch yourself doing this, stop it cold, and deliberately refocus on something more appropriate to your success in that situation? Make a habit of doing so from this moment forth.

It is not particularly difficult to do so. There are a number of ways to control self-talk, and they all begin with becoming more aware of when one is likely to start criticizing oneself and filling the mind with distractions and worries.

Once a negative thought is recognized, it can be stopped by saying "stop," either out loud or silently, then snapping the fingers or clenching the fist as a way of closing that thought off, then taking a deep breath to start all over. It can also be changed immediately to a positive thought. For example, if the voice speaks up, "I do not know if I can get up and block well today," it must be stopped, closed off and then followed with a strong, positively charged phrase like, "I can go as high as I want to any time, any place."

The key to cognitive control, then, is self-talk. Anytime a player thinks about something, he/she is in a sense talking to himself/herself. Self-talk becomes an asset when it helps an athlete stay appropriately focused in the present, not dwelling on past mistakes or projecting too far into the future. Self-talk becomes a liability when it is negative, distracting to the task at hand or so frequent that it disrupts the automatic performance of skills.

Controlling self-talk is a concrete skill for taking charge of one's mind and attitude and using them to help get ahead. Instead of letting the mind take them for a ride, players can get control and turn their minds into their best friends, their biggest fans and the greatest coaches on earth.

Positive Affirmations

The third skill in effective thinking is the use of positive affirmations. It is a fact that the way in which athletes think about themselves reflects the degree of their self-confidence and ultimately their behavior. Because athletes are only able to do what they think they can do, a strong belief in him or herself allows the freedom to use his or her full talents. A special type of self-talk that evokes these positive feelings and thus positive behavior is the use of affirmations. Affirmations are statements about something you want, phrased as if you already have it.

Phrases like "I am explosive and tireless" or "I want the ball when the game is on the line" or "My confidence is unshakable" are examples of affirmations. When used frequently (repeated many times a day or written many times a day) these statements promote confidence in the ability to do whatever action is being affirmed.

The most effective affirmations are both believable and vivid because they are phrased positively in the present tense and use the word "I." They capture the feelings of a particularly satisfying and successful experience: "My serve is a rocket," "I fly to the ball" and "I really come through under pressure" are all examples of positive affirmations. Note that each of these express a personal, positive message of something that is happening in the present.

> **Application Questions**
> 1. What are some ways in which you encourage your players to focus on their best attributes?
> 2. Interrupt scrimmages and other practice situations to ask a player what he/she is saying to him/herself just before serving or just before the start of a point. What other ways can you help players be aware of their self-talk habits?
> 3. Does each player on your team have a personal equivalent of "I am the greatest!" Do they each use this phrase to maintain confidence when the team is behind and beginning to struggle?

Perhaps the classic example of the power of an affirmation to affect sport performance is Muhammed Ali's "I am the greatest." While Ali's accomplishments in professional boxing are legendary, it is generally not known that as a young man of 16, Ali could be heard shouting, "I am the greatest!" from behind the wheel of his car as he drove down the streets of his hometown. Ali developed the belief that he was special years before he become the U.S. champion, the Olympic champion and the world champion and it was that belief which drove him to put in the long hours of roadwork, bagwork and sparring that were crucial to winning those championships. Every volleyball player owes it to himself or herself to develop their own personal equivalent of "I am the greatest!" and use it consistently, especially when the going gets rough and the fatigue starts to build up.

The most consistent finding in peak performance literature is the direct correlation between self-confidence and success. Everyone who has ever played or coached volleyball has seen a few truly confident players, the ones whom you would want to have on the court when the match is on the line. They are the players whom you do not give up on even when they have lost the first game, fallen behind or suffered an injury. Athletes who are truly outstanding are self-confident and this confidence is not an accident. Instead, it is the result of many years of consistently constructive, positive and effective thinking. This style of thinking enables these athletes both to retain and benefit from the experiences in which they have been successful and release or restructure the memories and feelings from their less successful experiences.

Consistent use of the three skills discussed here — selective perception, positive self-talk and affirmations — can help anyone develop higher and higher levels of confidence. The decision to search for individual potential is up to each of us. That decision can be avoided or embraced. An athlete can open up his/her mind and enjoy discovering what he/she is capable of or remain ignorant of the magic within.

Nate Zinsser, Ph.D., is a sports psychologist at the United States Military Academy's Center for Enhanced Performance. Robert Gambardella is the former head women's volleyball coach at the U.S. Military Academy, the current director of youth development and programs for USA Volleyball and a CAP Level III accredited coach.

The Psychology of Optimal Volleyball:
A New Look at Arousal and Performance

The Psychology of Optimal Volleyball: A New Look at Arousal and Performance

Nate Zinsser, Ph.D. and Robert Gambardella

One of the most frequently discussed topics in sport and performance psychology is the relationship between arousal and performance. Much has been written over the past decade on this subject and most coaches are familiar with the notion that each athlete and each team has their own "optimal level of arousal"—a specific degree of physical and emotional energy that brings out their very best play.

Customarily, this optimal arousal level is explained through the use of an inverted "U" model (see Figure 1), which illustrates how performance quality is affected by the performer's level of arousal. According to the inverted "U" model, performance improves as arousal increases up to an optimal point and then drops off as the level of arousal continues to increase. The model states that an "under-aroused" athlete will be "flat" and perform poorly due to a lack of energy or motivation, whereas an "over-aroused" athlete will be "nervous" or "over-adrenalized" and perform poorly due to an excess of energy that cannot be controlled. An athlete's best performances will occur under optimal arousal conditions where he/she is psyched up and energized but still under control.

An athlete's best performances will occur under optimal arousal conditions where he/she is psyched up and energized but still under control.

While useful in illustrating the folk wisdom that too much of anything will eventually yield diminishing returns, the inverted "U" model presents a very incomplete picture of the role of arousal in reaching peak levels of performance. This chapter will discuss the limitations of the traditional inverted "U" model and will offer a more functional view of arousal and performance. The next chapter in this section will further develop these points and will provide coaches with a framework for finding and maintaining that optimal energy zone throughout a volleyball match.

LIMITATIONS OF THE INVERTED "U" MODEL

One would assume that a behavioral model as widely published in the sport science literature and as widely accepted as the inverted "U" model would be based on research using athletes or other performers as subjects. In fact, the inverted "U" model was derived from data gathered on the performance of untrained, non-athlete subjects engaged in laboratory tasks with which they were unfamiliar (Freeman, 1940; Martens and Landers, 1970; Wood and Hokanson, 1965). This is a far cry from data obtained by skilled athletes engaged in playing a game they love and it may be inaccurate to generalize from these laboratory studies to the actual experience of athletes. To make matters worse, these laboratory studies were extensions of earlier research on motivation level and learning in animal subjects (Yerkes and Dodson, 1908; Young, 1936; Broadhurst, 1957). For example, Broadhurst (1957) demonstrated that rats learned to master a discrimi-

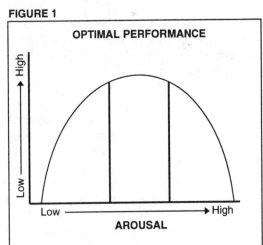

FIGURE 1
OPTIMAL PERFORMANCE

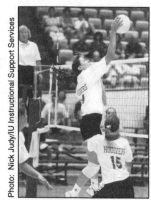

The reality of volleyball is that arousal levels vary significantly within a match, as environmental factors, the quality of the opponent's play and the player's physical condition take their toll.

nation task faster at moderate levels of motivation rather than at low or at high levels. Motivation was manipulated in this study by holding the rats under water for varying time periods to produce different levels of arousal and hence motivation for finding the exit from a maze. Extrapolating from the behavior of air-deprived rats to the reality of elite athletic competition, as has been done in many sport psychology writings (perhaps inadvertently), is both misleading and ineffective in coaching athletes to perform at their peak.

A second limitation of the traditional inverted "U" model is that it presents only a "snapshot" of an athlete's performance at a given arousal level. This creates the false impression that a player will attain a certain arousal level and the corresponding performance level and stay at those levels throughout a match.

The reality of volleyball, however, is that arousal levels vary significantly within a match, as environmental factors, the quality of the opponent's play and the player's physical condition take their toll. The element of time and its effects on both arousal and performance must be taken into account in any model that is to be useful to coaches.

Third, and perhaps most significantly, the inverted "U" model tends to cast arousal as a villain, as a force that will detract from an athlete's performance. Unfortunately, much of the sport psychology literature has confused the physical dimension of arousal — one's level of activation — with the psychological dimension of anxiety—one's level of fear and apprehension. The anxiety and sport competition anxiety inventories most commonly used by sport psychologists and coaches seem to measure the physical dimension of arousal rather than the psychological dimension of anxiety. For example, in the Sport Competitive Anxiety Test (Martens, 1977) only two of the 15 test items measure psychological state of mind (worry) prior to and during competition, while nine of the items refer to the physical dimension of arousal. In recent years, the authors of this inventory, in attempting to remedy this situation, have developed two separate measures, a cognitive anxiety and a somatic anxiety measure (CSAI-2, Martens, Burton, Vealey, Bump and Smith, 1982). This solution misses the point and continues to blur the distinction between anxiety and arousal. There is in reality no such thing as somatic anxiety. Anxiety is a cognitive effect; it is not somatic and in the opinion of the present authors, it is a mistake to try to present it as such.

...it is crucially important for athletes to treat the arousal that naturally occurs prior to and during a competition as a friend and ally who has arrived for the sole purpose of helping them reach new levels of performance.

Discussions of the inverted "U" are typically followed in sport psychology texts by descriptions of relaxation and tension reduction exercises designed to minimize the effects of arousal and bring an athlete "back down" to their optimal level. While well-intentioned, this advice tends to make athletes and coaches look at the arousal that naturally occurs before and during competition as something to be avoided and controlled, rather than something to be utilized and trusted. Doing so only undermines a remarkable natural system (the human organism) and encourages mediocrity rather than excellence.

A MORE FUNCTIONAL LOOK AT AROUSAL

If it is incorrect to treat arousal as a bad guy, how then should it be treated? We feel that it is crucially important for athletes to treat the arousal that naturally occurs prior to and during a competition as a friend and ally who has arrived for the sole purpose of helping them reach new levels of performance.

Arousal is characteristically experienced in the form of a racing heartbeat, jitters, sweaty palms and a queasy stomach. Each of these sensations are side effects of the human body's natural process of producing adrenaline prior to an important event. For athletes to be experiencing these sensations means that the body is producing adrenaline to make them stronger, faster, more alert and more reactive, all of which are very desirable qualities for an athlete. Arousal, then, or "nervousness," as it is commonly referred to, is really the impact of this adrenaline on the body, a clear signal that the body is doing exactly what it should be doing. Even though it produces some uncomfortable side effects in the form of stomach butterflies or shaky hands, arousal/adrenaline is a valuable gift to be appreciated and looked forward to by a player, rather than a curse to be fought off. Volleyball players should understand that it is "human" to become aroused at important moments and to experience that arousal through sensations usually labeled as nervousness. The inherent uncertainty of competition is exciting. This wonderful feeling is a major reason why people become athletes in the first place and the better the competition the more powerfully a player will feel it. Athletes must understand it is natural to be nervous and to be nervous is okay because this is the way the human animal was designed.

It all comes down to how each athlete chooses to look at and interpret his or her adrenaline/arousal. If we look at arousal as adrenaline naturally and marvelously sent to enhance performance in important moments, we see a fine-tuned machine deserving of our trust. If we view arousal as unnatural and dangerous, as an enemy that can destroy our effectiveness, then we see something frightening that needs to be driven away or tamed. To be effective, then, a player must learn to focus the mind while the body is nervous, excited and even highly aroused.

Being highly aroused is indeed unusual, but it is not abnormal. It may be distracting if allowed to be and it may even scare some athletes, but it does not need to. Therefore, being aroused must not be viewed as a problem. The feeling of being nervous must be enjoyed as a wonderful aspect of being human and being ready to play at a higher level rather than being seen as a signal that something is "wrong" with the body. The feeling of being "juiced" or "pumped up" will naturally take a player to a higher level of performance if it is trusted and allowed to take its course according to nature's blueprint. This view of arousal questions many of the assumptions behind the traditional inverted "U" model. Where the previ-

According to Zinsser and Gambardella, it all comes down to how each athlete chooses to look at and interpret his or her adrenaline/arousal. To be effective, a player must learn to focus the mind while the body is nervous, excited and even highly aroused. In return, the coach must give each athlete individual time to prepare for competition.

In the August/September 1992 issue of *Coaching Volleyball*, Vikki Krane, Ph.D., realized the importance of mental preparation and gives the following advice for coaches:

Providing time for athletes to prepare on their own is helpful. Build some time into your pre-competition warm-ups for athletes to do some individual mental readying. Some athletes will want to relax and calm down and be by themselves. Other athletes will stay close to teammates and get psyched up or perhaps joke around as a distraction from thinking too much about the game. It is important to get to know your athletes [as they should get to know the effects of their own arousal] and understand how each needs to prepare for competition. This will allow the coach to interact in an appropriate manner and, for example, avoid making comments that may make an athlete feel pressured.

(Krane Ph.D., Vikki. Minimizing anxiety. *Coaching Volleyball*, August/September 1992, 28.)

...coaches should explain to their players that their naturally produced adrenaline will only help them, and that this adrenaline, with all its unpleasant side effects, should be welcomed by players and looked forward to much the same way as they would look forward to a present on their birthday.

ous model would encourage an athlete to relax and bring down his or her arousal as soon as any nervous symptoms are detected, the present view encourages athletes to trust their natural arousal process and "ride" their adrenaline to new levels of performance.

Where the previous model implies that athletes tend to perform poorly because they are over-aroused, the present view sees poor performance as resulting from a lack of trust in the natural process of arousal, which stops athletes from becoming aroused enough to perform at their peak levels. While it is theoretically possible that a severe excess of adrenaline could create an ineffectively high arousal level, actual instances of this are extremely rare. Far more common is the situation of an athlete who, out of temporary discomfort or out of a mistaken perception of his/her arousal, deliberately fights the body's natural adrenaline production and winds up far below the optimal arousal level. To prevent this from occurring, we suggest that coaches explain to their players that their naturally produced adrenaline will only help them, and that this adrenaline, with all its unpleasant side effects, should be welcomed by players and looked forward to much the same way as they would look forward to a present on their birthday. Doing so will help greatly in fostering a more realistic and useful view of the effects of arousal on performance.

Application Questions

1. Ask your players to describe how they experience "nervousness" before a match. What symptoms do they typically experience? What do they say to themselves when these symptoms appear?

2. What advice could you offer to your players to help them learn to "love the butterflies" instead of dread them? How could you use your team captains or most experienced players or even a graduate from your program to help younger players learn how to utilize their adrenaline?

REFERENCES

Broadhurst, P.L. (1957). Emotionality and the Yerkes Dodson law. *Journal of Experimental Psychology, 54*, 345-352.

Freeman, G.L. (1940). The relationship between performance level and bodily activity level. *Journal of Experimental Psychology, 26*, 602-608.

Martens, R. (1977). Sport Competition Anxiety Test. Champaign, IL: Human Kinetics Publishers.

Martens, R., Burton, D., Vealey, R., Bump and Smith, D. (1982). Competitive State Anxiety Inventory-2. Symposium conducted at the meeting of the North American Society for the Psychology of Sports and Physical Activity (NASPA), College Park, Md.

Martens, R. and Landers, D. (1970). Motor performance under stress: a test of the inverted-U hypothesis. *Journal of Personality and Social Psychology, 16*, 29-37.

Wood, C.G., and Hokanson, J.E. (1965). Effects of induced muscle tension on performance and the inverted-U. *Journal of Personality and Social Psychology, 1*, 506-10.

Yerkes, R.M. and Dodson, J.D. (1908). The relation of strength of stimulus to rapidity of habit formation. *Journal of Comparative Neurology and Psychology, 18*, 458-482.

Young, P.T. (1936). *Motivation of Behavior.* New York: Wiley.

Nate Zinsser, Ph.D., is a sport psychologist at the United States Military Academy's Center for Enhanced Performance. Robert Gambardella is the former head women's volleyball coach at the U.S. Military Academy, the current director of youth development and programs for USA Volleyball and a CAP Level III accredited coach.

The Performance Dynamic: A Three-Stage Process

The Performance Dynamic: A Three-Stage Process

NATE ZINSSER, PH.D., AND
ROBERT GAMBARDELLA

The previous chapter in this section discussed the relationship between arousal and performance and challenged the conventional wisdom regarding this relationship summarized by the Inverted "U" model. Three limitations of this model were discussed: 1) it is not based on research using athletes or other performers as subjects; 2) it presents only a "snapshot" of an athlete's performance at a given arousal level and does not account for how arousal and performance vary throughout a long match; and 3) it tends to cast arousal as a villain or as a force that will detract from an athlete's performance.

Before the match, the coach acts like the driver of a championship team of thoroughbred horses, channeling the players' energies by giving them specific tasks to focus on, observing the condition of the terrain ahead and helping the players gradually get up into their "pace."

In order to foster a more realistic and useful view of the effects of arousal on performance, it was suggested that arousal and all the physical symptoms which accompany it (stomach butterflies, rapid heartbeat, sweaty palms, etc.), should be welcomed by players and looked forward to as a signal that they are now prepared to play at higher levels of intensity and precision. Doing so builds trust in the natural human body/mind and hence increases confidence, whereas the former view of arousal as something to be feared and controlled only inhibits this trust.

With this positive view of arousal in mind, we offer a different interpretation of the familiar inverted-U icon, which we refer to as the performance dynamic (see Figure 1). This model is designed to help coaches find and maintain the optimal level of physical activation and mental focus throughout a volleyball match. While the curve retains its familiar inverted-U shape and while performance quality is still represented on the vertical axis, the horizontal axis now represents the progression of time and not the level of arousal. As shown in Figure 1, this model consists of three stages: 1) a building stage in which the team establishes its control of the match through a combination of physical arousal and psychological focus; 2) a maintenance stage during which this control is sustained; and 3) an adjustment stage for regaining momentum when necessary.

PHASE I - BUILDING STAGE

The process of building toward a team's optimal performance begins days before the actual match. During this time, the coach acts like the driver of a championship team of thoroughbred horses, channeling the players' energies by giving them specific tasks to focus on, observing the condition of the terrain ahead and helping the players gradually get up into their "pace."

FIGURE 1

Phase 1: Building
Coach's Actions (key words - stick to gameplan)
a. Read the match.
b. Insist on staying with the gameplan.
c. Quick inventory of all players (starters and nonstarters).
d. Identify leader, winner and stabilizers that emerge.

Phase 2: Maintaining
Coach's Actions (key word - maintain)
a. Is the gameplan working? Change if needed.
b. Utilization of subs or time out to make tactical adjustments that will yield continual positive results.
c. Enthusiasm and emotion.

Phase 3: Adjusting
Coach's Actions (key word - focus)
a. Focus on problem areas.
b. Use of substitution.
c. Regroup, focus and re-establish gameplan with team.
d. Focus on weaknesses of opponents for us to attack.

As the match begins, the coach should be checking the scouting report to ensure the same lineup as in the scouting report. It is important for the coach to observe in the beginning of the match to make any tactical adjustments necessary.

An hour and 15 minutes before match time, the team reviews the scouting report of the opponent. At this point, the cognitive processes of what to do tactically should be rehearsed, so that each player has a specific image or concept on which to focus. The coach also emphasizes that the skills and techniques necessary for success against the opponent have already been mastered. After the scouting report is given, it is important to give the athletes five to 10 minutes of free time so that each player has time to process the key tactical points and see success with the agreed-upon game plan. This time is also necessary to allow each player to follow his or her own pregame ritual (sitting quietly, stretching, listening to a headset, etc.).

As the team moves on to the actual warm-up period, it is important that the coach stay close to the action. Here the "butterflies" and other nervous symptoms are likely to be their strongest, so the coach must be reassuring and guide the warm-up period so players feel they are in control of the situation. As the warm-up proceeds closer to the "5-5-2," the coach increases the volume and frequency of his/her comments to the team. During the "5-5-2," all team members, starters and subs alike should get quality reps. By this time, players are hopefully warm enough and focused enough so the exercise runs without a hitch.

As the match begins, the coach should be checking the scouting report to ensure the same lineup as in the scouting report. It is important for the coach to observe in the beginning of the match to make any tactical adjustments necessary. Does the scouting report fit with what is actually unfolding in the match? If so, stick to your plan. If not, take notes by rotation so that you can give some feedback when you get to that rotation. In essence, it is important to give your athletes a clear, concise picture of how the match is unfolding. If things are going the way you planned, keep giving them other tactical options to consider. If things are not unfolding as you expected, you need to ask yourself, "Would a substitution or time out enhance our play or could I make adjustments within the current line up (switching blockers, defensive positions, etc.)?"

It is important to be tactically oriented in this phase rather than to play on the player's emotions. Keep your thoughts, words, actions and body language positive and encouraging. A high level of confidence, positiveness and preparedness will give you the foundation that you will need to establish the desired momentum.

PHASE 2 - MAINTENANCE STAGE

At a certain point, the building elements will come together and the team will establish its momentum, rhythm and control of the match.

Coaches will know when this moment occurs more through instinct and gut feelings than by any objective criteria. At this point, the team's focus is on maintaining this momentum rather than building it further and the coach's behavior changes in order to facilitate this.

> It is important not to use the timeout as a plea to the players' emotions; all information that you want to in-process to the athletes has to be delivered in a low-key, relaxed manner. Doing so helps the team process the specific changes to be made in order to "turn the corner," and it also conveys, in an important nonverbal manner, that the coach has faith in the team's ability to regain dominance of the match.

This phase consists of the coach taking the gameplan and the "reading" of the match, and from this, deciding on how best to maintain the team's momentum. It is important to know which rotations will be most and least problematic. By this point the coach should have tactical plans ready to combat any changes that the opponent may attempt and can fine tune each rotation and maximize output by giving specific tactical instructions. The idea is to stay a step ahead of the opponent at all times (going from an "X" type offense to a "spread offense" or moving from a rotation to a perimeter defense).

At this stage, with momentum as support, the coach can also become more emotional. Capitalize on this momentum by rewarding good plays, good points and full effort with enthusiastic congratulations and support. Remind players of what they are doing well with specific positive comments about their position, anticipation and execution. If a side out or point is scored against the team, continue to show enthusiasm without communicating concern or worry ("That's OK! We've got 'em! Pour it on!") Most importantly, let them play and play hard! To help the team get the feel of this aggressive, sustained momentum mindset, include wash drills twice or three times a week in practice.

As shown in Figure 1 by the circle at the top of the curve, all the coach's behavior during the maintenance phase is focused on keeping the team within a relatively narrow range of play—its very best.

PHASE 3 - ADJUSTMENT PHASE

Should the momentum of the match suddenly turn, a new coaching phase is entered. When events turn in favor of the opponent, the coach must take immediate action, using time outs and/or subs, to "stop the train" momentarily and ensure that players are focused on what they want. During these timeouts remind the players of what was working well for them previously and which specific cues they need to refocus on in order to regain control of the match. If the coach feels that the team has exhausted all tactical moves, the time out has to be used to refocus their thoughts to what they need to do to change the course of momentum.

It is important not to use the timeout as a plea to the players' emotions; all information that you want to in-process to the athletes has to be delivered in a low-key, relaxed manner. Doing so helps the team process the specific changes to be made in order to "turn the corner," and it also conveys, in an important nonverbal manner, that the coach has faith in the team's ability to regain dominance of the match. The coach must remain confident in the team and show this confidence through body language (uncrossed arms and legs, face directed toward the players, body inclined forward) and carefully chosen, positive language. This is where the team needs the coach's fullest support; any expression of disappointment or anger will decrease that support.

By making comments short and concise and choosing the right language, the coach can refocus the players' attention back on to the sights, sounds and feelings that the team experienced when things were going their way, and thus develop the foundation for continued success. Keep the focus on only one tactical switch at a time; players are likely to be tired and frustrated at these times, which means that too much information presented too quickly can easily overload them and produce confusion. The key task in reclaiming momentum is staying focused on the desired outcome and not allowing the players to become discouraged or angry that their lead has been cut or lost.

It is important to stress that one's approach to the athletes at these times is critical. Players are likely to feel self-conscious and disappointed when they feel that momentum and possibly the match is slipping away, so it is crucial for the coach to convey trust and belief. The coach's display of confidence is critical (body language, verbal and non-verbal communication of trust in the players' abilities), whereas showing frustration can lead into disastrous results.

During timeouts, coaches must remind the players of what was working well for them previously and which specific cues they need to refocus on in order to regain control of the match.

Photo: University of Nebraska

Application Questions

1. How do you help your team "psych up" prior to a match? Do you lead the process or do you let the players guide themselves?

2. What are your key coaching actions to help get your team successfully through the "building phase?"

3. During a match, what techniques do you use to maintain your team's performance when they are playing well?

4. How do you recover your team's enthusiasm and energy when the momentum turns against you?

SUMMARY

There are certainly many factors that influence the momentum of a volleyball match. Some of these factors, such as luck, the opponent's physical condition and the opponent's skill level, are beyond a coach's control. Despite these factors, there is much that can be done to guide players before and during a contest, keeping in mind the three phases described above and the different coaching behaviors that are important in each phase. The coach's role in establishing and maintaining momentum is well summarized in a quote from the great Japanese coach Matsudaira, and in the commentary that follows it: Matsudaira, whose team won the Olympic gold medal in 1972, once said, "I find potential players with my eyes, pick them with my decision, improve them with my hands, and then build them to my design."

He is correct in the assumption that coaches plot the course even before they step on the court. The coach has a significant impact on his or her team. Chart the course, direct any changes that may occur and weather the storm together.

REFERENCE

Suwala, Lorne, Ed. (1977). *Winning Volleyball.* Canadian Volleyball Association.

Nate Zinsser, Ph.D., is a sport psychologist at the United States Military Academy's Center for Enhanced Performance. Robert Gambardella is the former head women's volleyball coach at the U.S. Military Academy, the current director of youth development and programs for USA Volleyball and a CAP Level III accredited coach.

The Attentional Demands of Volleyball

The Attentional Demands of Volleyball

IRADGE AHRABI-FARD, PH.D., AND
SHARON HUDDLESTON, PH.D.

The game of volleyball is predominantly an environmentally open sport which requires the athlete to attend to and react to various situations. The success of actual skill performance depends on early recognition of the development of the play, prompt transition and change of body position to the court area where ball handling would occur, and finally the execution of correct technique for an effective contact. Spectators typically judge performance by the effectiveness of the contact and therefore provide feedback based on the outcome of ball handling. Coaches should realize, however, that it is the pre-contact phase which determines the success or failure of the execution of the skill. The preparation (pre-contact) phase of skill performance in volleyball is more lengthy, more complex and places greater demands on attentional abilities than the actual ball handling process.

Spectators typically judge peformance by the effectiveness of the contact and therefore provide feedback based on the outcome of ball handling.

Understandably, the ability to control/switch one's attentional focus and to concentrate on relevant cues is mandatory. A player who is not trained to concentrate during the pre-contact phase will demonstrate jerky movements and late reactions to various game situations. Since an uninterrupted attentional focus before contact is the key component to optimal skill performance, coaches should place greater emphasis on the preparation phase that is necessary prior to contacting the ball.

NIDEFFER'S THEORY

In order to determine the specific attentional demands of the sport, it is necessary to consider Nideffer's (1976) work in the area of attentional style. He proposed that an athlete's attentional width during competition can range on a continuum from narrow (one or two cues) to broad (several cues) and that attentional direction can shift along a continuum from internal (cues inside oneself) to external (cues outside oneself).

A player who is not trained to concentrate during the pre-contact phase will demonstrate jerky movements and late reactions to various game situations. Since an uninterrupted attentional focus before contact is the key component to optimal skill performance, coaches should place greater emphasis on the preparation phase that is necessary prior to contacting the ball.

According to Nideffer, combining the continuum produces four distinct types of attentional focus and athletes must be able to switch from one to another as the game situation demands. The application of Nideffer's theory to the game of volleyball (especially the pre-contact phase) produces the following:

1. A narrow-internal focus that would be necessary for a player who is preparing to receive a hard-hit serve.

The athlete would need to relax the shoulders consciously in order to absorb the force of the serve. It would also be necessary for the athlete to check follow-through after contact to avoid adding force to the ball. A narrow internal focus would also be used for monitoring energy levels or

For a setter especially, concentration on the pre-contact phase of the skill of setting is more important than the contact phase, simply because this person needs to know the proximity of the hitters and the set-up of the blockers on defense in order to execute a successful set.

muscle tension during competition and for mentally rehearsing a skill such as the serve or a specific play prior to execution.

2. A broad-internal focus would be required of a setter when determining setting options during play.

This athlete must analyze the spikers' abilities and the abilities of the blockers at each point in the rotation in order to come up with the right offensive combination to divert attention and set the best option against the weakest blockers. This demands a broad internal focus while attending external cues.

3. A narrow-external focus would be required for a successful service reception.

The receiver would need to notice the distance of the server from the endline and the intensity of the server's movement prior to contact in order to predict the amount of force that will be applied to the ball. Early detection of the depth and the direction of the serve before the ball crosses the net will provide the receivers ample time to recognize their roles in the reception of the ball and move to the area for ball handling or support positioning. Total concentration on the movement of the ball and adjusting one's stance prior to contact would be the last important step in the pre-contact phase.

4. A broad-external focus would be necessary for the correct response to several game situations.

A spiker, for example, would use this focus to attend to the quality of the pass to the setter in order to analyze the setting options available. This information would be valuable to the spiker for transition to the correct spot preparing for the approach. While focusing on the set, the hitter should also keep track of the blocker's movement to decide on the angle of the hit. At the same time, some attention should be allocated to the movement of the defense in order to spot open areas of the court. A broad-external focus would also be necessary for effective blocking. Blockers should pay attention to the quality of the service reception in order to anticipate attack possibilities. After noticing the development of the offense, the athlete's focus should then narrow in order to attend to the ball as it leaves the setter's hands. While moving into position, attention must switch once again to the movements of the attacker.

The actual blocking movements are the simplest movements in volleyball but the attentional requirements of reading and reacting makes blocking the most challenging task of the game.

A broad-external focus would also be required for the correction execution of defensive digs. The athlete should focus on the development of the offense while at the same time detecting the movements of the blockers. While keeping a medium position in one's assigned area of court coverage, the digger should analyze the quality of the pass and the set exactly as the blockers would. When the set is up and the designated spiker is selected, the defensive player should focus on the offensive behavior of the spiker. This is necessary in order to adjust

An athlete with the ability to use selective attention can actually choose which relevant cues to attend to while ignoring the irrelevant ones.

Chapter 12

one's position and/or body level toward the area of predicted ball handling. Once again, concentrating first on the pre-contact phase of the skill is more important than the contact phase.

CONCENTRATION AND SELECTIVE ATTENTION

Concentration and selective attention are also important components of the attentional capabilities of highly skilled athletes. Concentration can be defined as how intently and how long one can attend to what is important (Harris and Harris, 1984). Total concentration allows an athlete to "lock-in" on the important cues, thereby avoiding mental errors in performance.

An athlete with the ability to use selective attention can actually choose which relevant cues to attend to while ignoring the irrelevant ones. One example is when the offensive pass to the setter is not read well by the quick attacker; the result will be a mistimed approach. The middle blocker should recognize this cue as one that no longer requires attention and attend to his/her offensive options. Athletes with a highly developed ability to direct their attention focus in this way and "lock-in" on relevant cues are virtually distraction-proof. These athletes will perform consistently.

The supposition that attentional demand is necessary, especially prior to ball handling, indicates that players need to be trained for this type of behavior in the game. Devoting the entire practice menu to the repetition of contacts is a very ineffective method of developing highly skilled volleyball players.

COMMON ATTENTIONAL PROBLEMS

During every volleyball game, an infinite number of stimuli (cues) compete for the athletes' attention. Some of these cues are relevant to performance and others are not. An athlete who allows her/his attentional focus to lock-in on irrelevant cues will experience a performance detriment (Harris & Harris, 1984). Since peak performance is achieved when athletes are able to attend to relevant cues and ignore those that are irrelevant, it is important that coaches spend some percentage of practice time identifying potential sources of distraction (irrelevant cues).

One of the main causes of the mental errors so frequently observed in sport is a shift from appropriate external cues to inappropriate internal cues. Even though the sport of volleyball requires that athletes be able to shift attentional focus as the situation demands, an inappropriate internal or self-focus can cause an athlete to miss crucial game cues.

Some examples of internal cues that will interfere with an athlete's game concentration are:

• High anxiety and/or fear will produce an uncomfortable feeling and athletes may attend to the physical symptoms of a pounding heart, increased respiration rate, dry mouth, an uneasy stomach and muscular tremor/tension.

• High anxiety and fear will also produce mental symptoms. Athletes may become occupied with their own negative self-talk (worry and self-doubts).

Once players have mastered the four types of attentional control, practice under increasingly more difficult and stressful situations is important. This is a meaningful step because one of the consequences of stress and becoming anxious is that players have a tendency to play their attentional strengths -- the ones in which they are most comfortable (Nideffer, 1993). Under pressure, the athlete will often revert ot the most comfortable style, which may not be appropriate for the situation. As anxiety reaches even higher levels, the players develop a narrow concentration field which is directed internally. This reaction often leads to the phenomenon known to coaches and athletes as "choking," where performance continues to spiral downward. The athlete fails to concentrate on the appropriate cues and instead focuses on feelings relating to failure. This negative spiral can be broken if they are able to refocus on the appropriate cues. Therefore, one of the most beneficial aspects of concentration training may be learning to refocus quickly and prevent a situation conducive to "choking."

Finally, there is another aspect of attention control training that coaches should be aware of. This pertains to the issue of individual differences. Just as some players can naturally jump higher or react more quickly, some players have a greater natural ability to control the direction and width of attention. However, all individuals are capable of effective concentration with appropriate learning skills and motivation (Nideffer, 1993).

(Mack, Mick. Attentional control: focus on success in volleyball. *Coaching Volleyball*, February/March 1995, 13.)

Coaches probably spend more time in broad-internal and broad-external foci than performers because of the nature of their job. Coaches are constantly assessing and analyzing their team's and players' situations in order to make the right moves at the right times. Obviously coaches, like players, can be affected by stress. Therefore, coaches need to be aware of the possible effects that stress may have on their concentrational capabilities. Coaches need to be aware of their own, as well as their athletes', attentional strengths and weaknesses. They should educate athletes about the differing dimensions of attention, help them acquire the skills and encourage them to practice concentration skills both on and off the court. Like physical skills, concentration is a mental skill that must be practiced in order to gain improvement.

Burke Ph.D., Kevin. Concentration training *Coaching Volleyball*, August/September 1993, 14.)

• Athletes who become angry may focus on plans of retaliation and miss the timely opportunity of selecting the proper behavior suitable to the game situation.

• Athletes might attend to, and as a result favor, a previously injured body part.

• Athletes may attend to feelings of fatigue or pain. Athletes who do not have the level of physical conditioning necessary for the entire contest will be distracted by their increasing feelings of fatigue.

• Athletes may attend to previous mistakes in ball handling and anticipate another mistake.

• Some athletes may become self-conscious regarding their uniform or certain aspects of personal grooming.

• Some athletes may think about personal problems. This will divert a certain portion of their attention away from the game.

EXTERNAL DISTRACTORS

Other causes of mental errors in sport can be categorized as external distractors. When athletes allow their attentional focus to "lock-in" on inappropriate cues in the sport environment, performance will suffer. Some examples of external distractions that will interfere with game concentration are:

• Crowd awareness can be a definite attentional problem for many athletes, especially if there is a significant other (parent, previous coach, boyfriend, or friends) in attendance.

• Verbal and non-verbal feedback, especially if it is negative, from the coaching staff can be a distraction for athletes.

• Verbal and non-verbal feedback from teammates, especially if it is negative, can break concentration on game cues.

• Athletes may be distracted by the behavior of the opposing players and coaches (intentional and unintentional psych-out).

• Athletes may focus on the effective responses and/or outstanding performances of the opposing players while ignoring their own roles.

• Athletes may be distracted by unfamiliar surroundings/facilities.

• Athletes may focus on the officials, especially if poor calls are made.

• Athletes may take themselves out of the game by watching it like a spectator rather than a participating player.

In addition to the inappropriate internal and external stimuli already discussed, coaches cannot ignore the possibility that some players will simply have a poor ability to concentrate.

In addition to the inappropriate internal and external stimuli already discussed, coaches cannot ignore the possibility that some players will simply have a poor ability to concentrate. Concentration can be defined as the length and intensity of one's attentional focus (Cox, 1990). It is one thing to be able to select relevant cues during competition, but if athletes cannot "lock-in" or concentrate on these cues, performance will suffer.

Once athletes have been warned of potential distractions and learn of their own attentional weaknesses, strategies for dealing with concentration and attentional focus problems can be practiced. The coach can identify individual problems through careful observation of the circumstances under which performance errors are made, private consultations with each athlete and through the use of Nideffer's Test of Attentional and Interpersonal Style (1976). Best results, however, can only be achieved when the coach incorporates this information into practices in game-like situations.

According to the authors, crowd awareness can be a definite attentional problem for many athletes, especially if there is a significant other (parents, previous coach, friends) in attendance.

REFERENCES

Cox, R.H. (1990.) *Sport Psychology: Concept and Applications*, Wm.C. Publishers.

Harris, D.V. and B.L. Harris. (1984.) *The Athlete's Guide to Sports Psychology: Mental Skills for Physical People*, Leisure Press.

Nideffer, R.M. 9176.) Test of attentional and interpersonal style. *Journal of Personality and Social Psychology, 34,* 397-404.

Iradge Ahrabi-Fard, Ph.D., is the head women's volleyball coach at the University of Northern Iowa (Cedar Falls, Iowa) and is a member of the *Coaching Volleyball* Editorial Board. Sharon Huddleston, Ph.D., is an associate professor and sport psychologist at the University of Northern Iowa.

Cue Recognition Training

Cue Recognition Training

IRADGE AHRABI-FARD, PH.D. AND
SHARON HUDDLESTON, PH.D.

The game of volleyball contains two types of skills — environmentally closed and environmentally open. The serve is the only skill which is environmentally closed. Since the server initiates the action with a toss of the ball, this skill is considered to be self-paced. Optimal performance of environmentally closed skills demands that the athlete limit movement to only that which is absolutely necessary and that it is done the same way for each execution. For the most part, however, volleyball is an environmentally open game. The athlete must react to a game environment which changes quickly (player and ball movement). Highly skilled volleyball players learn to adapt a well-learned skill (e.g., the forearm pass) to the movement of the ball (flight path, spin and speed) in order to produce a desired outcome (e.g., a pass to the setter). Correct execution, therefore, depends on recognition of the relevant cue (e.g., motion of the ball) and initiation of the necessary pre-contact movement. Without early cue recognition and the ability to concentrate on that cue, optimal performance in the game of volleyball is impossible.

Without early cue recognition and the ability to concentrate on that cue, optimal performance in the game of volleyball is impossible.

Attentional demands for early cue recognition differ for the two types of skills. Environmentally closed skills should be practiced with a narrow focus. The server, for example, should use a narrow-external attentional focus to decide upon the target area of the opponents' court and for the actual execution of the serve. Parts of some skills (e.g., the approach for the spike) may be practiced in an environmentally closed drill set-up with a narrow-internal focus.

Players should practice environmentally open skills with a broad-external focus prior to actual contact. All ball handling skills are environmentally open skills and should be practiced as such. For the coach, this means that the majority of practice time should be devoted to cue recognition and pre-contact movement drills (game-like) rather than closed repetition drills. This is not to negate the need for adequate repetition of closed skills such as the approach in spiking or other movements. Ball handling techniques and movements should be repeated correctly and adequately so that they do not place any demands on the players' attention.

In order to train athletes to respond successfully to the attentional demands of volleyball, coaches need to incorporate the principles already discussed into practice drills which closely approximate game situations. Each drill should provide athletes an opportunity to sharpen not only their skills but also their ability to recognize and respond to specific game cues correctly. To accomplish this, the coach should stress the pre-contact phase of skill execution. More often it is the pre-contact phase (cue recognition, speed of response and movement preceding contact) that determines the success or failure of the actual contact.

DRILL DEVELOPMENT

Presenting a comprehensive list of drills is not within the scope of this chapter nor would it be possible to do so for all types of teams.

Any coach should be able to create appropriate drills for her/his team

Effective concentration is characterized by: 1) focusing on one thing at a time; 2) focusing on present factors; 3) selectively attending to particular factors while at the same time not attending to other factors; and 4) complete involvement in the task. In order to be able to control our concentrational focus, it is helpful to understand how our attentional processes operate. Robert Nideffer has argued that an athlete's focus of attention varies along two dimensions: width and direction. Whereas width can range from broad to narrow, the direction of attentional focus can be either internal or external. The term broad represents a wide focus of attention. An athlete with a broad focus of attention is aware of many elements in a sport situation. An athlete with a narrow attentional focus is focusing on only one or two things at a time. Whereas the broad focus is thought to be a passive concentrational focus in which information is accumulated, the narrow focus is the active component in which action plans are generated.

If an athlete or coach has an internal focus of atttention, he/she is focusing on his/her own thoughts or images. An athlete or coach with an external attentional focus is concentrating on the elements in the sport environment.

(Burke Ph.D., Kevin. Concentration. *Coaching Volleyball*, April/May 1993, 31.)

During service reception, athletes should focus the distance of the server from the endline and intensity (speed) of the server's movement preceding contact. An intense narrow-external focus on the movement of the ball prior to crossing the net will allow the receiver ample time to move to the ball handling area.

based on the skill, experience level and specific attentional problems of the athletes. There are, however, a few points to remember when developing drills:

• Environmentally open skills should be practiced with an external focus which is broad for the pre-contact phase and zooms to a narrow focus immediately prior to contact. Athletes should be focused on relevant cues.

• The serve (environmentally closed) should be practiced by repetition drills with a narrow-external focus. Movement should be limited to only that which is necessary for execution and it should be consistent for each execution.

• Concentration should be intense at all times to avoid missing a relevant cue. If a cue is not recognized the instant it appears the opportunity for response will be gone.

• During service reception, athletes should focus the distance of the server from the endline and the intensity (speed) of the server's movement preceding contact. An intense narrow-external focus on the movement of the ball prior to crossing the net will allow the receiver ample time to move to the ball handling area.

• When executing the defensive dig, the athlete should begin with a broad-external focus to determine the position of the setter and type of set that she/he will be forced to use. While keeping a medium position in one's assigned area, the focus should now be switched to the attackers and the formation of the blocking unit. Immediately preceding the spike, the digger should be in a low floor defensive position with a narrow-external focus on the spiker and the ball. During the contact, the narrow-external focus should switch to the setter.

> Mental practice will be necessary if athletes display any of the following problems: easily distracted by irrelevant cues (internal or external); inability to locate relevant cues; high-anxiety responses; inability to switch attentional focus; or inability to concentrate for long periods of time.

• When spiking, athletes should use a broad-external attentional focus to perceive the quality of the pass to the setter and for analyzing the setting options available. During the approach, it is necessary to switch the focus to the ball as well as the movement of the blockers and the defensive coverage. Immediately prior to contact, focus should narrow to the ball to avoid net fouls and in order to react to the possible blocked ball.

• For blocking, the attentional focus should also be broad-external. Blockers need to attend to the quality of the pass to the setter in order to determine setting options as well as the position of the setter prior to contact. While moving into transition blockers should be aware of their blocking partner, the net and the spiker's strengths. During contact, the blockers should narrow their focus to the ball in order to be able to react to deflection or a tip.

MENTAL PREPARATION

Mental work on concentration and selective attention may need to be done in addition to attentional focus work in practice.

Mental practice will be necessary if athletes display any of the following problems: easily distracted by irrelevant cues (internal or external); inability to locate relevant cues; high-anxiety responses; inability to switch attentional focus; or inability to concentrate for long periods of time. Attentional training is as important as physical practice and conditioning activities and, therefore, should be scheduled separate from regular practices. Mental training and/or practice should be done in a quiet room, away from distractions, three to five times per week for 15-20 minutes each session. Positive results will usually be noticed within two to three weeks of practice. Although there are many concentration/attentional focus techniques from which to choose, the authors have found the following to be powerful tools:

- Breath relaxation technique is an easily learned stress reduction skill for high anxiety athletes. The athlete should be seated comfortably with eyes closed and instructed to focus first on the sound of their own breathing. After five to seven minutes the focus should be switched to the movement of the chest, attempting to allow the chest to fall deeper on each exhalation. The total time for the technique should be approximately 15-20 minutes. The athlete will soon learn to "trigger" relaxation with one deep breath. The technique will also enhance one's ability to concentrate due to the single cue (breath) focus.

- Practice with a yantra (Harris and Harris, 1984) will help athletes learn to switch their attentional focus from internal to external and will increase their ability to concentrate. A yantra is a 12" x 12" piece of black poster board with a white 2" in diameter circle glued in the center. The yantra should be placed in front of the seated athlete at about eye level. The athlete should be instructed to focus passively on the yantra (center) until the vision begins to blur. Next, instruct the athlete to close the eyes and visualize the yantra. After one to two minutes of visualization, instruct the athlete to once again open the eyes and focus on the yantra. These two steps should be repeated several times until the athlete has practiced a total of 15 minutes.

- Ball concentration (Harris and Harris, 1984) is a powerful technique that will accomplish the same results as the yantra through the use of a volleyball. The technique can be practiced individually or as a team. Place a volleyball in front of the seated athletes. Instruct the athletes to focus intently on the ball and to notice everything about the ball (i.e., shape, seams, stem, writing, scuff marks, etc.). After a couple of minutes, instruct the athletes to close their eyes and visualize themselves doing anything they wish with the ball. Allow several minutes to pass before instructing the athletes to open their eyes to focus one last time on the ball. The total practice time

Visualization is a mental training technique that involves seeing actual life experiences through the mind's eye. As humans, we are naturally visually oriented and vision provides a tremendous amount of stimulus information to assist in our reaction to environmental stimuli. The structure of how we "think" is visually oriented. And, the visual references made within the mind's eye are directly related to physiological arousal and stress reaction. The regular use of visualization can alter how we interpret stimuli, making it more positive or negative [i.e., the relaxation response and elevation of stress, respectively.] Because visualization creates an experience that is similar to the actual physical experience, our reaction to physiological arousal and stress reaction during visualization and the actual physical experience are similar (Klinger, 1980; Kosslyn, 1980; Sheikh, 1983, 1984).

Visualization cannot substitute physical practice, but if an athlete is physically proficient in a skill, research has suggested that mental practice is better than no physical or mental practice at all. If visualization is intermeshed with physical practice, it is more effective than either mental or physical practice alone (Felt and Landers, 1983); Weinberg, 1981; Corbin, 1972; Silva, 1983).

(Mills, Brett. Seeing through the mind's eye. *Coaching Volleyball*, December/January 1995, 30.)

> Attentional training is as important as physical practice and conditioning activities and, therefore, should be scheduled separate from regular practices.

should be approximately 20 minutes. Following practice, athletes can discuss their visualization experiences.

SUMMARY

The game of volleyball is a very demanding, environmentally open sport. A consistently high level of performance is not possible without specific attentional training. The majority of practice time should be devoted to cue recognition and pre-contact movement rather than closed repetition drills. Diligent mental practice inside and outside of the physical practice setting will produce confident athletes who are able to select, lock-in on and react quickly to the crucial relevant cues.

REFERENCES

Harris, D.V. and Harris, B.L. (1984). *The Athlete's Guide to Sports Psychology: Mental Skills for Physical People*. Champaign, Ill: Leisure Press.

Iradge Ahrabi-Fard, Ph.D., is the head women's volleyball coach at the University of Northern Iowa (Cedar Falls, Iowa) and is a member of the *Coaching Volleyball* Editorial Board. Sharon Huddleston, Ph.D., is an associate professor of psychology at the University of Northern Iowa.

Lessons for Coaches

Lessons for Coaches

PETER HASTIE, PH.D.

It has often been stated that coaches who demand more from their players and set higher standards will produce more successful teams. Researchers in physical education have verified this expectancy effect. It has been shown that teachers have expectations for pupils' performance (either overtly or covertly) and that students are able to detect these expectations. However, the expectations are not always positive. In cases where the teacher perceives the student to be of limited ability or potential, that teacher's interactions with the student are often counterproductive to good results.

Nevertheless, a factor of greater importance relates not to the standards that the teacher or coach sets up with a class or a team, but the standards that the teacher or coach actually accepts. Consider the case where a group of players is practicing service reception. The stated task is for a pair of players to pass until they have made 10 perfect passes (the criteria being that the setter can jump set the pass, taking only one step). One group is having difficulty and taking longer than the coach had planned for this drill. While some of the passes are meeting the criteria, others are being lobbed into the net so the setter has to move. While the setter can still jump set the ball, he/she needs to take a couple of steps to reach the ball. The coach, having recognized that valuable practice time is slipping away, sees a good but not perfect ball and calls out to the setter, "That one is O.K.; you could have set the middle."

In such a case, the coach has effectively changed the real task for the players. No longer do the players need to pass to a specific place at the net; rather, they now only have to pass at a height where the setter can jump set.

Consider another case of service reception. A drill is underway where the players are practicing receiving jump serves. The coach designates the criteria for a perfect pass—"a ball that goes directly or within one step of a designated player." As with the previous drill, the players are required to stay as passers until they make 10 perfect passes. If the coach continually praises a player's effort to save a hard serve from hitting the floor, even though the pass was not "perfect," the coach has effectively changed the stated objective. Thus, the real task in this situation has changed to moving quickly for the ball and appearing to be put in a complete effort to make a save rather than the successful performance of the skill.

There are two key factors relating to teachers' (or coaches', in this instance) expectations:
- the performance a coach actually accepts and rewards define the real tasks in teams; and
- the strictness of the criteria a coach uses to judge performance has consequences for task accomplishment.

Thus it is only the tasks for which players are held accountable that they tend to treat seri-

A coach must set high standards that he/she will only accept. Lowering standards of performance only serves to weaken players.

Coaches may be well-intentioned, but if they accept less than their stated goals, they should not become frustrated with the players when they reduce the quality of their responses.

In their 1992 study, Everett, Smith and Williams indicated, "Social loafing is said to occur when people exert less effort while performing a task in group settings than they do performing the same task alone." The old adage "many hands makes light work" is therefore only partially true when social loafing is present. Social loafing is a recognized phenomenon whereby an individual's efforts decrease as the number of team members increases.

Why does social loafing occur? Carron (1988) stated four potential reasons for the presence of social loafing. First, since an individual's contributions are frequently dependent on the work of others, maximum effort occurs less often in team sports. Secondly, lack of personal accountability is prevalent in groups. Thirdly, some individuals perceive the other team members to be more capable than themselves and therefore the value of their own contribution is limited. Finally, capable members do not want to continue to carry the burden of the capable–but less productive–members.

(Eide, Carolyn. Social loafing and volleyball. *Coaching Volleyball*, October/November 1995, 30.)

ously. If no expectations are required or any performance is accepted, then few players will actually attend to the content. Coaches may be well-intentioned, but if they accept less than their stated goals, they should not become frustrated with the players when they reduce the quality of their responses.

LEVELS OF ACCOUNTABILITY

The rewards/reinforcements given by coaches define the evaluative climate of a team and this climate relates to player accountability. Coaches can hold players accountable at three levels: 1) participation, 2) effort and 3) quality.

ACCOUNTABILITY FOR PARTICIPATION

While holding students accountable for participation may indeed be the major goal of many teachers in physical education, it is unlikely that coaches in a sporting context will need to attend to this factor. However, coaches will still need to set and reinforce standards concerning the starting time of practice sessions, practice uniform and other tasks such as preparing the net before training and shagging balls during drills.

ACCOUNTABILITY FOR EFFORT

Accountability for effort will often be the case where coaches are attempting to increase players' fitness, or perhaps during the early stages of defensive drills. In these situations, the player is rewarded if he/she makes an attempt for the ball, even if the ball is not touched.

ACCOUNTABILITY FOR QUALITY

Most coaches would propose that they are keen to produce quality actions from their players. Indeed, nearly all competitions are won by the teams producing the highest level of skill. However, it is not difficult for a coach to reinforce effort rather than quality during a drill. This can occur if the coach believes that the task is too difficult, or more commonly, where the coach is attempting to be positive and encouraging with the players.

TYPES OF ACCOUNTABILITY

Accountability can be either formal or informal. In physical education, formal accountability is the system of accountability that affects grades and informal accountability is that part which does not directly affect grades. Examples of formal accountability in volleyball include match results and the statistics taken on player performance, while examples of informal accountability include the coach's praise to players, allowing certain players to finish a drill early for good work, or conversely, making a group of players continue a drill until they reach a certain standard. The selection of a team to attend a national championship presents a powerful example of formal accountability for players in a team setting.

SUMMARY

The rewards for good performance or the consequences of poor performance are of course a salient part of the accountability system that coaches use in maintaining the work level of their teams. Thus the concepts of "rewards" or "consequences" might also be considered as having a significant effect on player involvement in volleyball. However, the extent to which players value the coach's instruction, feedback and accountability strategies, (that is the credibility the coach has with the players), will affect the way they interpret the accountability strategies operating on the court. If coaches do not demonstrate consistency in their accountability strategies, or they are not sincere towards the needs of players, the players may be less likely to be respondent to these strategies.

Questions Every Coach Should Ask of Themselves

1. Do you hold your players accountable for the following tasks?
   - A. Practice
     - Are they on time?
     - Early advice if they cannot attend?
     - Is there a definite starting time?
   - B. Dress
     - Do you train in uniform?
     - Are the players required to wear any special gear?
     - Are the players expected to be changed prior to starting time?
   - C. Equipment
     - Are players expected to put up the net and get the volleyballs, etc., without being told repeatedly?
     - Is there a consistent layout of training equipment?
   - D. Behavior
     - Do you have a code of behavior for players?

1. Do you use formal accountability techniques during training sessions?
   - A. Fitness
     - Do you record scores for fitness drills?
     - Have all scores been made readily available for players?
     - Have standards of performance been made public?
   - B. Skills
     - Do you keep statistics during training?
     - Do you use statistics during matches?
     - What happens if players are slack in keeping score?

3. At what levels do you hold players accountable during skill development?
   - A. Participation
   - B. Effort
   - C. Quality
   - D. Standards of Performance
     - Praise effort when quality is required?
     - Drop your standards during a difficult drill?
     - Allow players to finish a drill when they have done only six or seven when they are expected to complete 10?

Peter Hastie, Ph.D., is an assistant professor in the Department of Health and Human Performance at Auburn University in Alabama.

Maximizing Your Leadership Style

Maximizing Your Leadership Style

CAROL GRUBER, PH.D.

There is no question that coaches play a central role in structuring the athletic experience for their student-athletes. The behavioral decisions coaches make, as well as the attitudes and values they impart, directly affect both the performance and satisfaction of their athletes. The leadership role that coaches take with their teams is an important one, involving both influence and negotiation. Coaches are viewed as role models and mentors by athletes, parents, spectators and other members of the community. As such, most coaches feel a great need to influence their teams in ways to bring about the most positive experience attainable.

Recent research in the field of sport psychology suggests that certain styles and behaviors may be more effective than others in bringing about desired performance outcomes and greater team and individual satisfaction. Additionally, we know that it is not just coaching styles and behaviors that are important, but it is also how these are perceived by the athlete that becomes the crucial factor (Smoll and Smith, 1989).

Let us look at the concepts of "coaching styles" and "coaching behavior." What kind of styles and behaviors do we each possess and use in our interactions with athletes? How do we as coaches determine whether or not our leadership styles and coaching behaviors are bringing about the desired outcomes? What can we do to further enhance the athletic experience of the young people whose lives we touch on a daily basis?

LEADERSHIP STYLE

Generally, coaches possess and exhibit a variety of leadership styles and behaviors during their interactions with individual athletes and with the team as a whole. First, let us distinguish between "style" and "behavior." According to Webster (1986), style suggests a distinctive manner of expression. Style is a global descriptor which refers to a collection of more specific behaviors. A coach's style may be more or less authoritarian, or democratic in nature. The authoritarian coaching style is characterized by rigid rules and strong disciplinary action, a clearly defined hierarchy of authority and little input by team members with regard to team goals, practice sessions or team strategy. The coach is the primary decision maker for team matters and believes that the coach's central responsibility for the program makes it necessary to maintain ultimate control over athletes' competitive lives.

In contrast, the democratic coaching style lends itself to participatory decision making, a demonstrated concern for the individual, as well as the group experience, a positive and supportive rather than punitive communication style and a sense of shared responsibility for team outcomes. Most coaches fall on a continuum somewhere between absolutely authoritarian and decidedly democratic.

LEADERSHIP BEHAVIOR

Because leadership styles are so general in nature, it is more useful to look at specific behaviors exhibited by coaches and how those interface with situational and team factors. Such things as the level of competitive

There is no question that coaches play a central role in structuring the athletic experience for their student-athletes.

Research indicates that there is no one style of leadership which is always "best." On the contrary, effective leadership behavior is that which is appropriate for a specific situation and which takes into account the "performance level" of the people you are leading.

Performance level is a function of an individual's or group's willingness and ability to do an activity, ranging from low (P-1) to high (P-4). The more motivation, skill and responsibility they demonstrate, all other things being equal, the higher the level of performance. For example, a P-4 group or individual shows a strong desire to accomplish the task and has the necessary knowledge and experience to succeed. These people can be depended on to do an outstanding job.

People may perform effectively in relation to a particular task at a particular time, but their performance maybe at a lower level in other areas or at other times. Consequently, your choice of leadership style must vary according to the other person's performance level for each specific assignment.

(Bailey, Robert S. (1988). Center for Creative Leadership. In *Critical Thinking on Setter Development*, 1995,154.)

A coach must ask what kinds of behaviors are exhibited most often and whether or ot they receive the kind of athlete responses they are seeking.

maturity of the team, the type of sport, years of coaching experience and prior won/loss records change the complexion of the team and may call for different leadership approaches. Five specific leader behavior dimensions have been identified as being most used by coaches in the sport setting (Chelladurai and Saleh, 1980). Coaches find that a combination of the behaviors found below provide fairly accurate descriptions of their personal coaching styles.

As coaches, we must ask ourselves what kinds of behaviors we exhibit most often, and whether or not we receive the kind of athlete responses we are seeking. As stated earlier, the two most common ways of evaluating leadership effectiveness are through performance outcome and expressed satisfaction of both individuals and the team as a whole.

If we first look at how perceived coaching behaviors affect performance outcome, several observations can be made. Coaches who are perceived by their athletes as possessing more democratic and less autocratic behavior, a high level of training and instruction behavior and significant rewarding behavior, tend to be coaches with successful career records. Coaches who are perceived to use an overabundance of social support behavior instead of training and instruction behavior tend to be less successful (Fry, Kerr and Lee, 1986; Garland and Barry, 1988; Pratt and Eitzen, 1989; Weiss and Friedrichs, 1986). Greater team satisfaction is related to perceived levels of coaches' rewarding behavior and greater levels of training and instruction behavior (Chelladurai, 1984; Weise and Friedrichs, 1986).

> Coaches who are perceived by their athletes as possessing more democratic and less autocratic behavior, a high level of training and instruction behavior and significant rewarding behavior, tend to be coaches with successful career records. Coaches who are perceived to use an overabundance of social support behavior instead of training and instruction behavior tend to be less successful.

IMPLICATIONS FOR COACHES

What does this mean for today's coach who is concerned about how the team performs, as well as with how satisfied team members are regarding their athletic experience? Several possible strategies include:

1) Take time to evaluate your own coaching behaviors and those of your assistant(s). What are your athletes' perceptions of your coaching behaviors? Do your perceptions match your athletes' perceptions regarding your coaching style?

2) If your athletes' perceptions are considerably different than your own, take a look at the specific discrepancies and seek ways to minimize those, as well as to maximize behaviors that lead toward increased performance and greater satisfaction.

3) Provide a high level of the following behaviors to your team:
   • Emphasize instruction in skills and techniques appropriate to individual levels of readiness.
   • Clearly communicate the roles and responsibilities of each team member as they relate to the team objectives, making sure to outline the consequences for inappropriate behavior.

• Facilitate demanding and vigorous training techniques and practices.

• Carefully structure and coordinate team practices for maximal benefit to all.

• Ask for athlete input regarding group goals, practices and strategies, while clearly communicating that this input will be taken into consideration as you make decisions in those areas. Use your team captain to facilitate this.

• Provide specific and intermittent positive feedback for good performance of both individual and team skills.

4. Annually reevaluate your perceptions and those of your athletes to determine areas of greater or less concentration.

Please note that these strategies are not a fool-proof recipe for successful performance or maximum satisfaction, but a guideline for facilitating greater opportunities to reach these goals. Individual differences and situational variables make every team different and therefore must also be taken into consideration. As you choose to use some or all of the above ideas, you can be assured that you are attempting to create the kind of athletic environment which will provide a positive and productive experience for your athletes.

REFERENCES

Chelladurai, P. (1984). Discrepancy between preferences and perceptions of leadership behavior and satisfaction of athletes in varying sports. *Journal of Sport Psychology, 6*, 27-41.

Chelladurai, P. and Saleh, S.D. (1980). Dimension of leader behavior in sports: Development of a leadership scale. *Journal of Sport Psychology, 2*, 24-35.

Fry, L., Kerr, S., and Lee, C. (1980). Effects of different leader behaviors under different levels of task interdependence. *Human Relations, 39*, ii12,1067-1082.

Garland, DJ., and Barry, J.R. (1988). The effects of personality and perceived leader behaviors on performance in collegiate football. *The Psychological Record, 38*, 237-247.

Pratt, S.R., and Eizen, D.S. (1989). Contrasting leadership styles and organizational effectiveness: the case of athletic teams. *Social Science Quarterly, 70, 2*, 311-322.

Small, F.L., and Smith, R.E. (1989). Leadership behaviors in sport: a theoretical model and research paradigm. *Journal of Applied Social Psychology, 19, 18*, 1522-1551.

Webster, Merriam. (1986). *Webster's Ninth New Collegiate Dictionary.* Springfield, MA: Merriam-Webster, Inc., Publishers.

Weiss, M.R. and Friedrichs, W.D. (1986). The influence of leader behaviors, coach attributes and institutional variables and performance and satisfaction of collegiate basketball teams. *Journal of Sport Psychology, 8*, 322-346.

Carol Gruber, Ph.D., is the director of student services at the University of Iowa in Iowa City.

Leadership practices commonly employed by coaches in American sport are firmly based on the older psychological, sociological and business management theories. The pessimistic views of humanity depicted by the Freudians see humans as instinctual aggressive and dominating animals, while the behaviorists describe humans as malleable and passive victims of their environment, which determines their behavior. The sociological structural-functional school, which is not so different from Freudian and Behavioristic models, focuses on human adjustment and adaptation to society, not determiners of their own fate. The more optimistic symbolic interactionists posit a "free will" stance of human behavior. It is through choices that "reality" becomes significant. This model affirms that humans can think, are rational and are in control of their own situations; they are in control of their destiny.

(Miller, Martin G. Socialization via humanistic coaching. *Coaching Volleyball*, August/September 1993, 16.)

Momentum

Momentum

RICHARD BENNETT

Have you coached a match where everything suddenly starts to jell for your team? Your hitters are pounding the ball, the back row is digging every return and the serves are near perfect. On the opposite side of the net, mass chaos reigns supreme.

The opposing players are scrambling and out of sync, bad passes seem contagious and the serve seems to find the bottom of the net every time. Your squad is pumped and excited, ready to take on the world while your opponents show fear and dejection as if waiting for the match to be over. One thing is certain—momentum is playing a significant role in determining the flow of the game.

Momentum is unique to volleyball because of the emphasis on teamwork. Nothing positive happens in volleyball without an assist from a teammate. The idea of viewing volleyball as "pass, set, spike" is basically accurate. A player has to receive a hard-driven ball, pass it fairly accurately to another player who then sets the ball to a hitter who attacks the ball across the net. Add two players who are attempting to block the original attack and another player covering for tips or roll shots, then you have the possibility of all six players contributing to the task of getting the ball back across the net in three preferred contacts. The nature of the game lends itself to the emergence of momentum at some time during the interchange of volleys.

Momentum tends to occur more often when players are properly psyched up and willing to give total effort.

What causes this phenomena of momentum which seems to have such an important effect on the outcome of the match? It seems to be caused by a combination of factors including an increased flow of adrenaline, an inspired level of play, the right mood of the players, a certain natural competitiveness and sometimes even luck.

How do you get momentum? No one really knows. What is important is learning how to keep momentum once you have it.

Momentum tends to occur more often when players are properly psyched up and willing to give total effort. If everyone is committed to being the best that they can be at all times, despite adverse circumstances, then momentum is more likely to happen spontaneously. At the same time, there are a number of conditions which run counter to the impetus of momentum and which definitely should be avoided. The challenge for coaches and players is to be aware of these conditions and to follow prescribed guidelines to ensure that momentum is not interrupted, or at least only minimally affected. The following points will prove helpful in accomplishing this goal.

> Momentum is unique to volleyball because of the emphasis on teamwork. Nothing positive happens in volleyall without an assist from a teammate.

DEAD TIME

This is probably the most significant interrupter of momentum. The 30-60 seconds needed to process a timeout usually hinders the tide of emotion needed to sustain momentum. The coach needs to keep the team together and emphasize continued total effort, minimizing the chance for

According to Bennett, one unhappy player on the court can instantly destroy any potential for building momentum.

a let-down. Timeouts also are especially effective in breaking a string of good serves. When a timeout is called, the server has time to think about making a mistake, not to mention the added pressures which naturally builds in the huddle. Coaches should avoid mentioning the significance of the serve while in the huddle.

The three-minute break between each game can also destroy any hope of maintaining momentum. In an effort to maintain that competitive edge, coaches should have their squad waste little time in switching sides and huddle together near the team bench. What this ensures is the maintenance of a bond between the players while the coach submits the line-up for the next game.

SUBSTITUTION

One of the secrets to successful coaching is to know when to make effective substitutions.

When things are going well, it is appropriate for the coach to continue using the players who started the match. The group has managed to perform effectively and has aspired to a certain anticipated level of success. Switching the lineup just for the sake of making a change can drastically affect the quality of teamwork and, eventually, momentum.

A coach's worst fear is to make a substitution to provide on-court experience for a player, only to have that decision backfire when it negatively impacts momentum.

Oftentimes when the starter(s) reenter the game, it is too late. The team finds it difficult to get back into the flow of the game and loses its competitive edge. The coach should establish definite substitution patterns so that players are not surprised when they are substituted. Examples are service for designated players on the second rotation and good defensive specialists for spikers in the back row.

LETDOWNS

Mistakes and poor play will inevitably happen at some point during a match for any team. Coaches need to stopgap this by not allowing their players to get down on themselves when mistakes are made. One unhappy player on the court can instantly destroy any potential for building momentum. If a player cannot be encouraged to believe in him/herself, that player should be immediately replaced by someone who is familiar and comfortable with the starting team. The same rule applies for a good player who berates a teammate, and in turn, negatively affects teamwork and the potential for building momentum.

OPPONENT'S PLAY

Often an excellent play by your opponents, such as a key block or save, is enough to stem the tide of momentum. Coaches should prepare for this possibility by pointing out that the team welcomes good competition and the potential great plays which accompany good teams. Your players should be inspired by great plays, not intimidated by them. Encourage them to feed off the energy and enthusiasm generated on the other side of the court to their advantage. Never giving up is the watchword.

INJURY

No one welcomes the possibility of injury, especially to the star player. Teams have a tendency to let the loss of a great player drastically affect their play. At this stage, momentum can be quickly interrupted and difficult to regain. Players must accept the increased responsibility and pressure, and challenge themselves to raise the level of their game. This shift in roles can maintain momentum and bring a team closer to victory.

SUMMARY

In conclusion, momentum is definitely an important aspect of the game of volleyball. It affects the flow of the game and has a real impact on the outcome. It is caused by a combination of emotions and events which continually occur throughout each game. An understanding of the possible causes and means of maintaining it can greatly enhance team play and assist the coach in making the right decisions during the course of the match.

Richard Bennett is the head girls' volleyball coach at Heidelberg High School in Heidelberg, Germany, and is a USA Volleyball CAP Level II accredited coach.

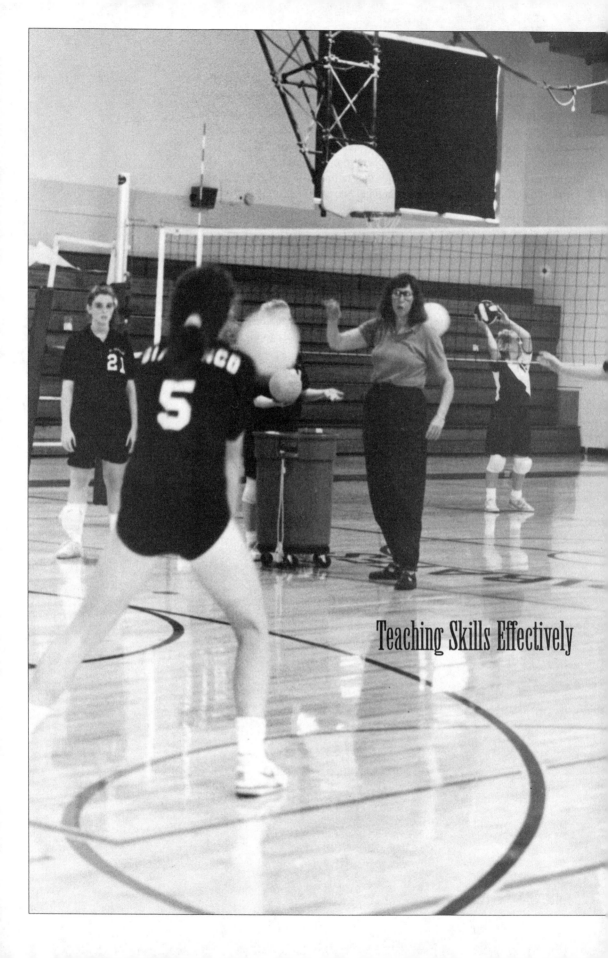

Teaching Skills Effectively

Teaching Skills Effectively

LISA KOWALSKI

A very important part of our job as coaches is being an effective teacher. This is especially true when teaching players a new skill. We must be efficient in this area if we want our players to have a good skill base.

There are many teaching techniques that can be used. Modeling, using pictures, giving verbal cues, teaching the feel of the movement and giving feedback are all essential elements in the learning process.

MODELING

Many coaches spend too much time talking about how the skill should be performed instead of showing it. Words are often misunderstood and while the coach might have one thing in mind, the players may hear and interpret it differently.

Since 83 percent of all learning occurs through sight and only 17 percent through other senses (Boyce, 1991), it is not surprising that modeling plays such an important role in learning. Lirgg and Feltz define modeling as "A general process in which observers attempt to reproduce the responses exhibited by another person" (Lirgg and Feltz, 1991).

Who should be the model? Research has shown that the best model is a coach who is able to perform the skill correctly (Landers and Landers, 1973; Lirgg and Feltz, 1991). In Lirgg and Feltz's research, they compared teacher versus peer and skilled versus unskilled models. They found the group that observed a skilled teacher performed the best; the second best was the skilled peer; the third best was the unskilled peer and the group that performed the poorest observed an unskilled teacher. The conclusion could be drawn that a coach should not demonstrate a skill unless he/she can do it correctly.

A coach has other options if he/she cannot demonstrate. Someone else can demonstrate, perhaps an older, more experienced player or a film or video could be used.

USING PICTURES

Another resource we have to teach skills that is not used very often is pictures. The saying, "a picture is worth a thousand words" can be applied to learning motor skills. Displaying a series of pictures of a certain skill provides a unique advantage over a video or a live model. The learner can move at his/her own pace by deciding when to add a new item of information, rather than watching a video or live model that may move too rapidly. The coach can also freeze frame a certain aspect of the skill that he/she wants the learner to see (Juaire and Pargman, 1991).

ATTENTION GIVING VERBAL CUES

Coaches and teachers agree that attention is critical to both learning and performing motor skills (Hill, 1991). Hill identifies two different types of attention: automatic and controlled (Posner and Snyder, 1975; Schneider and Shiffrin, 1977; Hasher and Zacks, 1979). Automatic attention requires minimal energy and little or no awareness occurs. Controlled attention, on the other hand, requires active mental energy and it

Only if a coach is an effective teacher can players learn new skills properly.

Coaches should present volleyball skills with visual cues as an integral part of the presentation. Include key visual cues when explaining situations. When dialoguing with a developing player, suggest that at the time of service the player focuses in a "tight square area" where contact will occur with the hand of the server and the ball, once quickly scanning foot, hip and shoulder position. By following the ball's trajectory after contact until it passes the net will provide other pieces of meaningful information.

Construct practices so that advanced visual information can be gleaned as early as possible for every drill/situation. By using the concept of temporal occlusion, vary practice settings. The coach might use the words "shut" and "open" to refer to eyes open or eyes closed. Close the eyes immediately after the server presents the ball to the toss of the ball to the highest point (pre-contact) and after contact (post-contact) to the ball passing the net.

(Kluka Ph.D., Darlene. A new technology and field test of advanced cue usage in volleyball. *Coaching Volleyball*, October/November 1995, 23.)

According to Kowalski, the advantage of having the ability to interpret internal information is that the players can coach themselves.

interferes with other mental activities. It happens slowly because it uses "serial processing," which means it can only process one thing at a time.

An example of automatic attention is an experienced player attacking a ball. They do not have to think about which foot goes first or how to plant and jump. It is automatic.

A beginning player, however, must feel overwhelmed because he/she must think about many things: approaching, jumping, swinging, contacting the ball, staying out of the net, all at once using controlled attention, which only processes one thing at a time.

This is why as coaches, we should not overload young players with too many stimuli when learning a new skill. They should only have to concentrate on one thing at a time. Also, it is important that we know the skills well enough to give correct cues and to give them in the correct order (Anshell 1990).

TEACHING THE FEEL OF THE MOVEMENT

Showing the skill through modeling and giving verbal cues focus on how the movement should look and be performed, but does not give attention to how it should feel. Coaches should teach players how to interpret internal information when learning a new skill (Boyce, 1991).

For example, when teaching the shrugging of the shoulders in blocking, show what muscles would be stretched and which are contracted and let them feel what it is like to extend the shoulders (internal cues). Set the net 20 inches lower and let them just stand and extend their shoulders and penetrate over the net. They can feel the extension and penetration without having to think about anything else.

> Feedback is another vital part of the learning process. Once the player has seen the skill performed correctly and has been given some verbal cues, he/she then tries to perform the skill. It is at this point that feedback is crucial.

The advantage of having the ability to interpret internal information is that the players can coach themselves. For instance, if they get used on a block in a match, they can ask themselves, "Did I feel my shoulders shrug?" and be able to answer the question without asking the coach. The time used in practice feeling the correct performance will be used as a frame of reference when performing the skill in competition.

The coach can really extend his/her imagination in this area. Any way the coach can manipulate the surroundings and the player to get them to feel the correct movement will enable the player to learn the skill more effectively.

GIVING FEEDBACK

Feedback is another vital part of the learning process. Once the player has seen the skill performed correctly and has been given some verbal cues, he/she then tries to perform the skill. It is at this point that feedback is crucial. Here are some of the things to remember when giving feedback:

1) Give it immediately. If you wait too long, it loses its effect.

2) Be positive. Tell the players what they are doing right, rather than what they are doing wrong.

3) Be specific. Use the verbal cues that were given during modeling.

4) Limit feedback to one cue at a time. Do not try to fix everything at once.

When training future players and lower-skilled players, modified equipment and rules should be used for both practice and game play. Modifications might include different balls, lower nets and shorter service lines. To encourage continued participation and motivation, all athletes/students must experience success or they will not continue to attempt the skill. The result is a lack of improvement in skill performance and game play.

(Harrison Ed.D., Joyce and Marilyn Buck, Ed.D. Volleyball instruction: results of using game and equipment modifications. *Coaching Volleyball*, April/May 1995, 13.)

SUMMARY

All of these elements are important to the learning process. As coaches, we should use each of them to assist our players in learning new skills.

REFERENCES

Anshell, M. (1990). An information processing approach to teaching motor skills. *Journal of Physical Education, Recreation and Dance, 61, 5*, 70-75.

Boyce, B. (1991). Beyond show and tell — teaching the feel of the movement. *Journal of Physical Education, Recreation and Dance, 62, 1*, 18-20.

Hasher, L. & Zacks, R. (1979). Automatic and effortful processes in memory. *Journal of Experimental Psychology. General, 108*, 356-388.

Hill, K. (1991). Pay attention! *Journal of Physical Education, Recreation and Dance, 62, 9*, 18-20.

Juaire, S. & Pargman, D. (1990). Picture memory: the use of pictures to teach motor skills. *Reading Improvement, 27*, 200-202.

Landers, D. & Landers D. (1973). Teacher versus peer models: effects of model's presence and performance level on motor behavior. *Journal of Motor Behavior, 5*, 129-139.

Posner, M. & Snyder, C. (1975). Attention and cognitive control. In R. Solso (Ed.) *Information Processing and Cognition*. The Loyola Symposium. Hillsdale: Erlbaum.

Schneider, W. & Shiffrin, R. (1977). Controlled and automatic human information processing: detection, search and attention. *Psychological Review, 84*, 1-66.

Lirgg, C. & Feltz, D. (1991). Teacher versus peer models revisited: effects on motor performance and self-efficacy. *Research Quarterly for Exercise and Sport, 62, 2*, 217-224.

Lisa Kowalski is the head women's volleyball coach at Belleville Area College in Belleville, Ill., and is a USA Volleyball CAP Level II accredited coach.

Section IV: Coaching Philosophy and Ethics

Commandments for Volleyball Coaches

Commandments for Volleyball Coaches
Karen Heinemann

To all experienced volleyball coaches: think back to the first year as a head coach. If it was anything typical, it included a combination of extreme highs and lows, extreme happiness and frustration and was constantly overshadowed by critical self-evaluation of personal coaching abilities. Ah, to have been able to coach then knowing what experience has brought now.

Undeniably, would not it have been nice to have had some basic guidelines to help run the volleyball program at that time? It would have been nice to have practical, "learned-in-the-trenches" guidelines. Look no further.

The less-experienced coach can glean a tremendous amount from the following 11 commandments for high school volleyball. In addition, however, the more-experienced coach can refresh a memory or two and apply these suggestions to a current team, no matter the level of play.

According to Heinemann, in order to have a successful season plan, coaches should emphasize the process needed to achieve the outcome rather than the outcome itself.

1: THOU SHALL HAVE A PLAN

It has been said, "If you fail to plan, plan to fail." How wise that person was! This can be applied to every facet of life, but especially to coaching. A less-experienced coach will quickly learn that quality coaching requires year-round planning. A plan for your program must be in place that includes where it is going and how long it will take to get there. This plan should be based on a series of goals (e.g., off-season goals, in-season goals, weekly goals, individual practice goals and individual match goals). Personally, I advise not measuring these goals in terms of wins or losses. Doing that would put the emphasis on the outcome. It is more important to emphasize the process needed to achieve the outcome. That can be done by using more tangible measures (e.g., percentages of serves to target, passes to target, kills, blocks, successful sideout plays, etc.). I believe this because too many times teams may win despite playing below their capabilities and other times they may lose, even though they played at their optimal level.

2: THOU SHALL MAINTAIN A CLEAN, SAFE PLAYING ENVIRONMENT

This will help set the atmosphere for the job you and your players have to do.

3: THOU SHALL BEFRIEND THE JANITOR

His/her help could prove to be invaluable to you. If your equipment breaks, you need a fan or need help with a P.A. system, you want this person on your side.

4: THOU SHALL READ AND KNOW YOUR RULE BOOK

A coach will never know how important this is until a situation arises when you need to know instantly if a call was correct. Most officials are

A coach and a team must have fun and enjoy the sport.

conscientious and try hard to make correct decisions. I do not believe in arguing a judgment call, no matter how much I might disagree. However, I have been in situations where a rule was ignored or interpreted incorrectly and I have had to defend my objection to the call (but always in a nice and controlled manner). Case in point: I once had two players who, right before they interchanged, always touched hands. In one match, an official called them for overlapping because their hands were touching on the serve. Very nicely and under control, I had to point out to the official that the rule for overlapping is only concerned with the parts of the body that are touching the floor. Unfortunately, this particular official was not aware of this and refused to change the call, even after being shown the rule in the book (which I keep next to me on the bench). However, this was an exception to the rule and most officials will correct themselves if they are incorrect.

5: THOU SHALL EDUCATE YOUR PARENTS

Many parents know little or nothing about the sport of volleyball. You can save yourself a tremendous amount of aggravation and frustration if, at the beginning of pre-season training, you have a parent meeting. Explain to your parents the game, the techniques, the tactics and most importantly, the rules.

6: THOU SHALL UTILIZE YOUR PARENT'S TALENTS AND ENERGIES

> ...the bottom line is for you and your team to have fun and enjoy the sport. It is particularly important that you be able to laugh at yourself. Contrary to what many coaches believe, your players will have more respect for you if they are allowed a glimpse of the human side of you.

Most parents will jump at the opportunity to play an active part in their child's interests. They can be of great help to you for things such as fund raising, transportation, match statistics, scorekeeping, linespeople and videotaping.

Also, you will quickly recognize those parents who are better kept occupied during matches. There are the parents who mean well, but are a little overzealous in vocalizing their opinions to officials, players and coaches. If kept occupied during play, it will help make the match a more positive experience for everyone involved.

7: THOU SHALL KEEP A SENSE OF HUMOR

This is critical if you desire longevity in the coaching profession. Granted, you want to establish an atmosphere of seriousness and purpose when your team is practicing or playing. But the bottom line is for you and your team to have fun and enjoy the sport. It is particularly important that you be able to laugh at yourself. Contrary to what many coaches believe, your players will have more respect for you if they are allowed a glimpse of the human side of you. So remind yourself to laugh next time you accidentally miss the bench when sitting down after a timeout or sit in water from a leaky bottle or get hit in the head by an ill-aimed spike. Your blood pressure will stay down and you might even get a few good anecdotes for that end-of-the-season sports banquet speech.

8: THOU SHALL KEEP AN OPEN MIND

Go to as many clinics and workshops as possible and be prepared to hear differing opinions at each one. Keep yourself receptive to new ideas. One of the beauties of this sport is that it is dynamic and ever-changing. The most successful coaches are the ones who are imaginative and innovative enough to develop systems specifically for their team's abilities and level of play.

9: THOU SHALL RESPECT YOUR PLAYERS

Make an effort to get to know your players personally. The more you know what makes them tick, the more successful your season will be. Show you care about them both in and out of the gym. Always treat them with respect. And, when stopping to eat on road trips, always let them go first. This is for your own bodily safety.

10: THOU SHALL ALWAYS BE POSITIVE

Positive thinking is an excellent cornerstone on which to build your program. It has staying power that can help get you through those times when things just are not going right. Positive thinking is also highly contagious. If your team consistently witnesses your positive attitude in practice and during matches, it will become infected with the same positive energy and will accomplish more than you ever thought possible.

11: THOU SHALL REFER TO COMMANDMENT 10 AGAIN AND AGAIN AND AGAIN

No matter how much knowledge you have, no matter how much you prepare for your season, no matter how much talent your players have, there will always be times when things do not go your way. It is because we are dealing with people. The human element is a variable that will never be totally predictable. Because of this, there will always be disappointments, some big, some small. It is during these times that you must dig deep into your inner-self for the strength to keep doing what you feel is right. By consistently displaying a positive, enthusiastic attitude, your players will learn to hang in there and believe in their abilities.

You will also re-energize your own "batteries" if you make it a point to talk to yourself daily in a positive manner. Many times we are our own worst enemy when it comes to evaluating how we are doing. Granted, we want to be truthful with ourselves. But, we also need to be our own best boosters. We need to express and emphasize to ourselves the good things we are doing.

*Karen Heinemann is the former head girls' volleyball coach at Southern High School in Durham, N.C., and is a USA Volleyball CAP Level II accredited coach.

Coaches Should Keep Volleyball in Perspective

Coaches Should Keep Volleyball in Perspective

RENEE C. DE GRAFF

As opportunities in sport for girls and women increase, coaches must make a concerted effort to keep sport in perspective. Self-worth and self-esteem are often equated with an athlete's success on the field or court. Evaluation by coaches and parents often determines how athletes feel about themselves and how long they stay in their sport.

Junior volleyball clubs allow athletes to improve their skills in a fun and usually nonstressful environment. Successful coaches provide an opportunity to learn fundamentals and to gain playing experience. Many volleyball club players earn college scholarships. But why do so many players become so disenchanted with volleyball that after their college careers they take a few years off from competition?

Communication is the key to alleviating a number of team problems.

College players—especially those in programs that have high expectations and a strong tradition—often find that volleyball has gone from being fun to being a job. The players are considered workers who must perform and execute like someone involved in making a tangible product. This product, more often than not, is a championship.

But what happens to the players if these championship goals are not achieved? Some coaches become so focused on victories that they consider their players nothing more than cogs in a machine. If a cog malfunctions, it is quickly replaced. Individuality is suppressed for the betterment of the team or destructed and reconstructed to fit the mold of the machine.

Coaches should address players' technical and fundamental errors, not their personal attributes. The stronger players are often the targets of personal criticism; some coaches see them as court leaders who should make no mistakes. This added pressure is unfair. These athletes become scapegoats for team problems and setbacks. Coaches should help their athletes confirm their identity on the court through encouragement and empathy, rather than question their identity through criticism.

Communication can alleviate many team problems. Good coaches spell out their coaching philosophies during the preseason and listen to their players' ideas. It is imperative that coaches and players know each other's concerns. Time demands during the volleyball season should be discussed and coaches should understand the academic pressures their athletes face. Collegiate play marks the end of the volleyball road for all but a small percentage of players. An education is the best thing athletes can get from scholarships. Coaches should realize the long-term benefits of a college degree versus a championship. In the end, the one who benefits most from a championship is the coach. Players need degrees.

Each fall, only a few volleyball players earn the right to say they are national champions. But all volleyball players who give honest effort can hold their heads high. Athletes who do not play to win are not true com-

Does playing collegiate volleyball interfere with academic success? Not if the student-athlete comes to college prepared academically, with a supportive family environment and encounters a coaching staff concerned with academic success. Players should know that a coach is concerned about their academic success and wants their parents to be involved in their successes. Each player is still ultimately responsible for his/her own success, but each additional source of support makes that success more attainable.

(Laite, Berkley. Volleyball and academic success. *Coaching Volleyball*, August/September 1995, 22.)

petitors, but effort and desire cannot be measured by victories. Neither can personal commitment and contribution.

Coaches need to recognize the sacrifice that players make. The element of fun, which can be achieved through well-played matches regardless of outcome, should be a primary goal. Players should be leaving volleyball programs with positive self-esteem. If that were each coach's goal, then all volleyball players would be champions.

Renee De Graff is the former assistant women's volleyball coach at the University of Notre Dame and currently works in the marketing department of Gordon Food Services in Vandalia, Ohio.

Effective Communication

Effective Communication

KAREN GEE

"What was the call?" "Who touched the net?"

"SUUUB!!"

Are you going hoarse trying to talk to the officials who work your matches? If so, there might be a communication problem. Granted, nothing is going to make you feel better about a match that is poorly officiated. And since coaches have many things to worry about during a match, even a simple request like asking for a substitution can add to an already high level of stress.

What effect will this have on your evaluation of the official? The official may have called a perfect match, but if you do not know what calls were made or if you cannot even get a timeout, you are not going to think very highly of this individual's performance. This chapter discusses what coaches can do to improve communications with officials and what characteristics to look for in an official who has good communications skills on the court.

Coaches should be sure their playing captain understands the rules.

WHAT THE COACH CAN DO

First, be sure a school representative (i.e., assistant coach, administrator, etc.) introduces the officials to the line judges, scorekeeper and the statistics crew. With the ever-growing emphasis on statistics, referees can be very helpful if they are told to whom numbers should be given.

Second, coaches should request substitutions from their normal position on the bench whenever possible. Although most second referees will look for subs in between points, do not expect them to see you asking for a sub when you are at the end of the bench talking to your extra players.

Third, if playing in a crowded and noisy gym, it helps for coaches to stand when requesting a sub or timeout. This will save on the voice and standing definitely catches the official's eye.

Fourth, coaches often make it a habit to signal the first referee when asking for a sub or timeout. It is the second referee's responsibility to handle these tasks. Since the second referee is most often closest to the bench, make it a policy first to speak to the second referee. If this individual is distracted or handling a request from the other team, then signal the first referee to make sure your request is handled.

> Through the natural rhythm established during a volleyball match, the officials are on the alert for bench requests during a certain period of time between points.

Fifth, try not to ask for a sub or timeout just as the first referee is about to whistle for the serve. Coaches may not be heard in time to gain the psychological advantage of disrupting the server in this situation. Through the natural rhythm established during a volleyball match, officials are on the alert for bench requests during a certain period of time between points.

There are numerous debates concerning effective interactive behaviors between coaches and officials during competition which have the potential to influence the progress of the match. These behaviors combine for performance enhancement and match facilitation.

The best officials in any sport have achieved skill and rank over years of training, practice and study of the game. During that time, they develop a sense of professionalism that conforms to the ethical standards of sport.

The professional official protects the integrity of the sport to benefit the players and ensures that both teams are provided with an equal opportunity to win the match.

The coach also maintains professional standards defined by the profession. Victory is crucial to the success of any program. Skill development, teamwork, cohesiveness and personal growth are also very important factors to the coach and team. The coach is responsible for providing opportunities for the team to win.

During each match, the coach uses many techniques to influence the momentum to the advantage of his/her team. The coach is expected not to dishonor or embarrass the team, the university, the sport or the profession and is responsible for performance stabilization at a high level which, in part, is achieved by focusing attention on the significant aspects of the match. The coach assists the athlete in the processing of information leading to performance enhancement and stabilization at a high level. When both coach and athlete lose concentration, that performance breaks down.

(Polvino Ph.D., Geri and Terry Lawton, Ph.D. Interactive behavior between official and coach. *Coaching Volleyball* Special Issue, March 1994, 22.)

When it is time for the next point to begin, both prepare to do their respective jobs by focusing on the court. Their attention is no longer on the bench, thus making it difficult to see a coach seeking a last-second timeout.

Finally, coaches should be sure their playing captains understand the rules. Time after time a coach has sent the captain over to me with a question. When the call is explained to the player, it is obvious from the expression on the captain's face that he/she did not know the rule. Apart from yelling across the court, the captain is your means of communicating with the first referee. Coaches need to take advantage of it by educating their players on the rules of the game.

WHAT THE OFFICIALS SHOULD BE DOING

Officials have two main tools with which they communicate during a volleyball match. Those tools are their whistle and their hand signals. Assuming that a referee's judgment is satisfactory, imagine what the match would be like if the individual did not use either of those tools or used them improperly!

Coaches have the opportunity to evaluate officials. Aside from their own personal opinions in regards to the match, coaches can use the evaluation as a means to point out specific areas where improvement in communication is needed.

Here is a quick checklist:
- Does the referee have a weak whistle that is hard to hear?
- Can you tell by the tone of the whistle that a sub or timeout is being requested?
- Is the whistle being blown promptly? Is the reaction time good?
- Do the officials use the correct signals for the calls that they make?
- Do the officials hold their signals long enough for coaches to see what the call was?
- Are both officials using the same signals and working as a team?
- Do the referees have demeanors which allow the captain to approach them without feeling intimidated? Do they handle questions courteously and efficiently?
- Are the officials attentive to both benches in between points?
- Does the first referee make use of the second referee and line judges? Does the first referee even look at the other match officials for assistance?

SUMMARY

When volleyball officials are evaluated for their NAGWS National Rating, approximately 30 percent of their score is based on communication skills. If every call were correct and there were no mistakes on the part of an official, this individual would still be perceived as having called a bad match if they were not able to communicate decisions to coaches, players and spectators.

Try some of the communication skills for coaches in your next match. And when evaluating an official, keep the above questions in mind and be more specific in your critiques. The payoff should be better officiating.

Karen Gee is the president of the Affiliated Boards of Officials.

Communication Can Give You the Winning Edge

Communication Can Give You the Winning Edge

LENORE SUAREZ AND
I.J. GORMAN

How many times have you heard someone say, "You are not hearing what I am saying!"? Effective communication has many barriers. A good idea presented poorly is ineffective communication. People tuning into how you say something may miss what you say.

Assistant coaches and athletes need to understand what the head coach is telling them. Assistants instructed privately have the opportunity to ask for clarification, but athletes coached in the gym may not. As a result, the coach's instructions should be as clear as possible.

When a coach criticizes an athlete's performance, it needs to be done with tact and sensitivity. Everyone has ways they prefer to hear that they are not cutting the mustard. Some athletes like feedback immediately and are not embarrassed by it. Others prefer to be told privately in a low and controlled voice. Still others want to know how their actions or behavior have negatively impacted the team. Coaches need to know how to communicate in a variety of situations.

When a coach criticizes an athlete's performance, it needs to be done with tact and sensitivity.

Establishing effective communication with and among a team and coaching staff can make the difference between winning and losing. All coaches have seen teams with great athletes that could win matches despite personality conflicts. But good communication can save frustration and tears, no matter what the talent or experience of the players.

Organizations use communication as a key factor in reaching their goals. Building the communication support system between coaches and athletes and among athletes themselves can help any program achieve its best season ever.

COMMUNICATION STYLES

There are four communication styles (based on Carl Jung's research on the subject) that can help a team to communicate more effectively. A short test can help to identify each person's communication style as that of either a thinker, a senser, an intuitor or a feeler; players can then be grouped according to their individual styles. Each type of communicator—thinker, senser, intuitor, feeler—handles day-to-day interaction and stress differently and each favors certain practices of thought and speech.

Thinkers

Thinkers analyze and synthesize before addressing a situation. They want to know a broad spectrum of information relating to a decision: the background, factors leading to the decision, how the decision is being carried out and how it will affect them. Thinkers like chalk talks and concepts.

Sensers

Sensers want facts and are not wordy. They like results. They respond to things they can touch, see and feel; they like things of an immediate nature. They tend to be action-oriented and are often valued for their ability to get things done. Sensers like action, not chalk talks.

Intuitors

Intuitors look to the future with a global perspective. They are good with concepts and often are able to relate diverse thoughts and ideas into

Members of a team can find comrades they might not otherwise bond with in the ready-made support group of like-minded people.

meaningful wholes. Most intuitors display good innovative ability and skill in looking at the "big picture." They are planners.

Feelers

Feelers are "gut reactors." Highly sociable, they are empathetic and understanding in their approach to others' needs and are able to discern what lies beneath the surface.

Persons within each group must get to know each other and then identify phrases and approaches that they prefer in critical situations. (For example, thinkers prefer to be asked their feelings about a situation only after they feel informed enough to discuss it—they do not like to give "gut level" feelings. So a coach, to communicate effectively, would need to explain strategies and skills more fully to this type of player.)

During these meetings, each person should anticipate becoming fast friends with others in the group because each has so much in common. Participants may find not only a ready-made support group, but also the tools to interact better with other types of communicators.

After identifying types, key phrases and approaches, coaches and players now have tools for supporting and approaching individuals from each group. Often, for the first time in a coach's varied years of experience, everyone had an approach that could reach each person. Rather than stereotyping personalities, players and coaches now remember which communication style each person has and can take advantage of that knowledge for the betterment of the team as a whole.

> ...personality conflicts are, at the core, really just communication style differences! By using an effective communication system, a coach can deliver information that the assistants and athletes will understand.

When potential problems arise during the season, things are not taken personally. Differences are attributed to communication styles. It is interesting to watch players who just a year before were so sensitive to criticism being criticized by teammates and acknowledging it as concern rather than reacting defensively. Personality conflicts will be at a minimum; people have the right to be different and this system allows for that.

After experiencing this revelation, players often feel that this new understanding of communication will also help them in the classroom. Most students have difficulty relating to at least one professor because they cannot understand him or her. Players often agree that the communication knowledge would help them, too, after graduation.

This suggests that personality conflicts are, at the core, really just communication style differences! By using an effective communication system, a coach can deliver information that the assistants and athletes will understand. This can help any coach, no matter the level, reach program goals. Learn not to let words or delivery hamper effective communication!

Lenore Suarez is the head women's volleyball coach at Principia College in Elsah, Ill. *I.J. Gorman is the former assistant volleyball coach at Principia.

Effective Timeout Communication

Effective Timeout Communication

WALT KER

You have just sent your team back on to the court after a timeout, the score tied 13-13. During the break, you told your players that the opposing team's setter usually dumps on the second contact after coming out of a timeout situation and that defensively your team needs to look for this. Nods of assurance are confirmation that your message was received. But as the next play progresses and the setter dumps the second ball, your defensive players are nowhere to be found.

As a coach you ask yourself, "Didn't I just say that was going to happen?"

Chances are you did. But was it the only point you stressed during the timeout? Or was it one of several pieces of information you were attempting to communicate to your players and its significance got lost in the shuffle?

This chapter will address effective communication techniques that coaches may utilize in timeout situations. Also, the chapter will examine timeout strategies that may be employed during competition.

Coaches can use several techniques to ensure an effective timeout situation.

A major mistake many coaches make, especially at the high school level, is the fact they do not keep notes for themselves as the match progresses. Keeping a brief set of notes during the match can assist the coach during a timeout situation in four ways.

• *Memory.* How many times have you walked into a timeout situation unable to remember what it was you wanted to stress to your team? Having a set of notes will provide a coach information with which to refer.

• *Prioritization.* Keeping match notes can help a coach pick and choose what information is most important and then relay it to the team during a timeout. Often times coaches will attempt to overload the timeout with too much information. For the athlete, it is difficult to listen and process all of this information. A coach should begin the timeout by stressing what is the most important thing to remember and the second most important thing to remember.

> Having a set of notes allows a coach to be very specific in their comments, eliminating the possibility of rambling. Many new coaches fall into this communication trap. Keeping notes helps you organize your thoughts as you prepare to emphasize a key point in the timeout.

• *Do Not Focus on the Last Event.* Too many times I have seen coaches spend 25 seconds of a 30-second timeout berating a player on what happened in the last event before the timeout was called. This action has little positive impact on the player and limits the opportunity the coach has to speak with their team. Remember, you may have only eight minutes in a two-hour match in which to advise your team effectively in making adjustments to any on-court situations. Thus, it is more time-efficient to stress the key points from your notes, not to reprimand a player for being out of position.

• *Specificity.* Having a set of notes allows a coach to be very specific in their comments, eliminating the possibility of rambling. Many new coaches fall into this communication trap. Keeping notes helps you organize your thoughts as you prepare to emphasize a key point in the timeout. Coaches need to be extremely efficient in important points of communication.

MAKE ONE KEY POINT

"Here is the one thing I want to talk to you about."

That is how I like to open timeout situations with my team. It helps the players tune into me, ready to listen for the one message —that one key point—that I am about to emphasize.

"Right now, their outside hitter is killing us down the line. Let's concentrate on setting a wider block and channel the attack inside."

At this point, coaches should reemphasize the same point, but in a different way.

"Let's set the block wide and dig cross-court."

There you have it. One point, no confusion. By repeating the information you have made it a clear-cut team focus.

At this juncture in the timeout, it is okay to deal with individuals to give them specific pieces of information (e.g., telling your setter to go to a particular hitter or demonstrating an error-correction technique for your right side blocker who is consistently being tooled).

It is critical for coaches always to bring the team back together before the timeout is over and re-emphasize the one key point (e.g., even ask your team what that key point is). This communication strategy should keep your team focused on what needs to be done as you send them back into the match.

EMOTIONAL AWARENESS

Coaches must have an awareness of the mental frame of mind their team will have when a timeout is called during a match. This frame of mind is typically driven by the team's momentum on the court when the timeout is taken.

• *Poor Momentum.* The players will use the coach as an emotional crutch. The coach must enter the timeout calmly, confidently and with a mentality that here is the solution. ("Team A just scored three points off of us, but here is how we are going to stop them.")

At this point, the players become great listeners. Be honest with them by accurately assessing the situation, but indicating a resolution. ("They are serving tough. But, here is how you are going to pass the ball better. Back up one step, step back and see the ball.")

Now, your players are fully aware of what needs to be done having been sent back on to the floor after the timeout with newborn confidence. Your own emotional state needs to reflect this.

• *Good Momentum.* In this situation, the coach should come off of the bench energized. Congratulate your players by telling them what they are doing well ("Super job setting the block. We are channeling the ball right to the diggers."). Through positive reinforcement, coaches can help their players feel good about themselves.

In regards to listening skills, your players are likely to be lousy listeners in this particular timeout situation. They are ahead in the match, performing successfully against the opposition and feel they do not need your help. Coaches should take advantage of this opportunity to make

Coaches must have an awareness of the mental frame of mind their team will have when a timeout is called during a match. This frame of mind is typically driven by the team's momentum on the court when the timeout is taken.

their players better listeners by providing positive feedback, thereby encouraging your players to continue playing at a specific level of efficiency.

DETERMINING WHAT TO SAY IN A TIMEOUT

Specific comments in a timeout should be affected by who called the timeout and who is serving. In all likelihood, the team who called the timeout is typically the team which is receiving serve.

•When Receiving Serve:

The coach should go in calmly and confidently with a specific agenda, emphasizing a key point which could include any one of the following areas:

1) Set selection. This could include a specific play or player.

2) Serve receive adjustment. Shift to a three-person or four-person serve receive pattern. (Perhaps a reference to body position, e.g, open up better).

3) Transition reference. (Reminder of defensive responsibilities after attack.)

The key is to get your team to think in the "right-brain" and get them into a competitive mode. Comments such as "see the ball," "let's go score a point," or "let's be aggressive," can prompt a team into thinking in a flow state—a non-analytical process whereby the athlete just "plays the game."

•When Serving:

The coach should again have a key point to emphasize. This could come from any of the following agenda items:

1) Opposing hitters. Information on where they hit, what kind of shots and how it will affect your block.

2) Set prediction. Who is the most likely attacker to be set by the opposition after the timeout.

3) Serve location. Tactics on where you want your server to place the ball.

4) Setter about transition. Where do you want your setter to put the ball on transition?

5) Defensive emphasis. Get your players to think about scoring out of the timeout.

Again, coaches should send their squad back on to the floor with a right-brain reference on what it is they are going to do (e.g, "dig a ball," or "see the hitter's approach").

IDENTIFY AND EMPHASIZE KEY COMPONENTS

Coaches should call a timeout when they feel they have identified a nugget of information which could most affect the outcome of the match. By calling a timeout, a coach can offer this advice to the team in hopes it will help them win the match.

During the timeout, a coach should not be afraid to repeat this important piece of information. It is also helpful to illustrate the same message, but in a slightly different way. The key is to let the players know it is a crucial point. Finally, emphasize the significance of the message in such

1. Successful communication means understanding that the person with whom you are communicating has had different experiences than you.
2. Everybody is an individual. Thus, the way you communicate with one person might not work with another.
3. Be aware of nonverbal communication.
4. Be consistent, clear and honest. Do not be sarcastic, belittling or degrading.
5. Communicate in a style that is congruent with your coaching philosophy and personality.
6. Be empathetic. Look at the situation from the players' perspective before reacting and show concern for them as people, not just athletes.
7. Create a supportive environment, one where athletes feel they are valued.
8. Be a good role model - lead by example.
9. Solicit input from the team (i.e. ask how things are going, what is going well, what is not, what do we need).
10. Many coaches have an open-door policy. If you do, make sure the players know you mean it!

(Johnston, Thomas and Valerie Wayda. Are you an effective communicator? *Coaching Volleyball,* April/May 1994, 29.)

Receiving messages from athletes is for some coaches a lost art. A coach can be an excellent teacher of skills but if he or she is unwilling or unable to listen to athletes, credibility suffers. Following are principles of becoming a better listener.

- Concentrate on listening. Give your players your full attention. Position your body and use eye contact to show you are listening.
- Search for the deeper meaning of messages. Be attentive to the athlete's body language. An athlete's looking at his/her feet while talking to the coach about a mistake might indicate a lack of self-confidence. This might be the coach's cue to encourage rather than scold the athlete for an error.
- Do not interrupt. Showing impatience downgrades your credibility. Coaches should repress emotional responses to athletes' suggestions and respond constructively. This conveys effective listening skills and also leaves a player's self-esteem undamaged.
- Ask questions. During conversations, ask athletes to clarify messages, paraphrase and repeat phrases and use bridging techniques such as head nods and saying "uh huh."

(Weiss Ph.D., Maureen and Diane Wiese. Motivating your volleyball players. *Coaching Volleyball*, December/January 1989, 10.)

a way that it becomes extremely important to the players. "If you do this, we will score."

SUMMARY

Coaches have a responsibility to be excellent speakers and to enhance their players' listening skills. But to accomplish this task, coaches need to practice timeout communication just as much as players need to work on spiking, digging and blocking.

Test yourself in practice. After finishing a mock timeout, have your assistant coach ask the players what they just heard. Compare their responses with your intention. This communication drill will emphasize to your players the importance of listening during a timeout.

Coaches can adapt this listening quiz into a live match scenario by asking their players what the one key point is before breaking the huddle. The players' responses, or lack of, will send a strong signal to you that your message is not getting across (e.g., no one on the team knows) or that some of the players are not listening (e.g., only several players do not know).

Another test is to have your assistant coach (if none, someone whom you respect) critique your timeout communication. Have a checklist of questions already prepared to assist the evaluation process (e.g., did you overload the player's with information? Were you rambling? Did you repeat and reemphasize the point?).

Assistant coaches should be trained to be effective timeout communicators. This is especially true in the event the head coach wants to speak privately with a particular player during a critical timeout. However, always remember to refocus the team before sending it back into the match by reiterating the one key point.

In time, coaches will see their message effectively getting across to their players, make better listeners out of each player and ultimately make a positive difference during a match.

*Walt Ker is the former head women's volleyball coach at Cal State Northridge.

Finding Friends in Coaching

Finding Friends in Coaching

MARILYN MCNEIL, PH.D.

"I have not been in contact with them [other coaches in the sport], but I know a lot of them. Coaches seem to be so busy in their own little worlds and do not communicate. I do not like it because you stop learning. That is frustrating. I have a few friends from coaching. A couple of them I talk to on a regular basis, once a month, maybe bimonthly."

"I see my high school coach once a year, at camps. I call two of my friends in coaching once a year. I do not feel I have many friends because I am so busy. My only friends are those I can call a year later."

Compare the aforementioned quotes by female head coaches in upper-level Division I women's sports to these responses to the same question by two football coaches at the Division I and II level.

"It is a physical sport and it is tough. You develop a bond with teammates that you never lose. You like and respect teammates that get things done correctly, friends for life. A group spirit, a group of players that want to prove to the coach."

Studies indicate female volleyball coaches find it more difficult to foster friendships with their peers than male coaches of other sports.

"Information is passed freely among coaches and programs, professional information and personal information. Every time I get a spare moment I will call a friend or coach. I call people I know once a week. Like recruiting, I do not like to get behind. Once a week, I pull out my address book and call two or three times."

Recent research has shown that coaches, regardless of gender or level of competition, are generally not very astute at maintaining friendships with peers in the coaching field. Friendships are crucial to human development as social beings, not as isolates.

According to Josselson (1987) identity is the "stable, consistent and reliable sense of who one is and what one stands for in the world." The gender identity literature has celebrated two different views of development identity. The major studies of male development (Vaillant, 1977; Levinson, 1978; Erikson, 1950) have found career, achievement and independence to be the principles of male identity development. Relationships are secondary. In the major studies of female development (Josselson 1987 and Gilligan, 1982) the role of attachment is paramount. Chodoraw (1978) explains that women, because they are mothered by someone of the same sex, never have to separate from their primary care giver the way males do. The male, in order to identify with his father, must separate from his mother. This pattern, argues Chodoraw, forms the beginning of the individuation development of the male and continues the attachment development for the female.

Play offers another look at the same phenomena. Lever (1978) studied fifth grade children at recess and discovered that girls play cooperatively and boys competitively. Girls' games are turn-taking, boys' are outcome-guaranteed. Face-to-face confrontations are common in boys' games and never end the game. Arguments will persist but solutions are found so that winners and losers are pronounced. Girls' games are dissolved if arguments persist. This, Lever argues, also adds to the ability of the boy to depersonalize competition and for the girl to develop sensitivity and feeling for others. Such depersonalization of competition by males al-

The author believes that coaches must strive to be friends with other coaches.

lows individuation to occur; such sensitivity by females allows attachment to occur.

This theory of gender identity is interesting if we return to the coaches' statements above. The football coaches are male and both show a distinct interest in maintaining and soliciting friendships. It also seems obvious that the football playing experience is a natural conduit for developing friendships that seem to become lifelong. This contradicts the gender theory espoused above: that males choose individuation as their hallmark. Now consider the quotes from the coaches of the female teams.

What is happening to female coaches? There seems to be a disregard for relationships, a non-caring for teammates or for coaching peers. The gender literature supports the attachment, the self-in-relation for the female, but the female coach is indicating self-alone identity. This concern might be partially explained by motivation theory. Research within this same study found that the female volleyball player has an intense desire to play for the coach, to please the coach. Two quotes from players are related here. "I practice to impress the coach, he's the one who decides who plays."

"Back of my mind, playing great for the coach. She makes all the decisions." This is extrinsic motivation. Motivation theory confirms that extrinsic motivators, once removed, remove the desire to continue the activity. Therefore, when the volleyball player finishes the activity, she has no reason to maintain the relationship. She resorts to her gender identity of self-in-relation, to her primary family relationships, not with her teammates or coaches. Interestingly, both female and male volleyball coaches of female teams were interviewed for this research and both reacted similarly. However, the male is reacting according to accepted male gender theory, self-alone. The female is contradicting gender theory on the surface; however, it was strongly evidenced throughout the interviews that family was the prime attachment concern for the female volleyball coach.

> ...on the surface, female coaches must create an environment that will develop lifelong, lasting relationships, where the game is played for the love of sport and not to please superiors.

Implications are many and there are more as this research moves in some other directions. But on the surface, female coaches have got to create an environment that will develop lifelong, lasting relationships, where the game is played for the love of the sport and not to please superiors. We, as coaches and administrators, must find a way to encourage players to maintain friendships with teammates, encourage coaches to maintain friendships with teammates who become coaches or coaches just being friends with other coaches. It may mean that in the future we will have a stronger body of female athletes who, as they mature, will remember their playing days better. It may mean that we can motivate these women to become generous and spirited alumni of our programs and institutions, instead of other charitable organizations, or institutions. Making friends has a lot of good for now and for the future, but like many projects for this gender, it is not an easy task.

REFERENCES

Chodoraw, N. (1978). *The Reproduction of Mothering.* Berkeley: University of California Press.

Erikson, E.H. (1950). *Childhood and Society.* New York: Norton.

Gilligan, C. (1982). *In a Different Voice.* Cambridge, Mass: Harvard University Press.

Josselson, R. (1987). *Pathways to Identity Development in Women.* San Francisco: Jossey-Bass.

Lever, J. (1978). Sex differences in the complexity of children's play and games. *American Sociological Review, 43,* 471-483.

Levinson, D. (1978). *The Seasons of a Man's Life.* New York: Knopf.

Vaillant, G. (1977). *Adaptation to Life.* Boston: Little, Brown.

Marilyn McNeil, Ph.D., is the athletics director at Monmouth College in West Long Branch, N.J.

Section V: Program Development/Management

Home Events: More Than a Game

Home Events: More Than a Game

PAM BRADETICH

When on a road trip, how many times, as a player or a coach, have you walked into a facility for your game or practice and wondered, "Where is the net?" or "Where are the balls?" And typically, the only person in sight who might be able to help you is the custodian! Have you ever thought maybe you were the only one to read the contract?

The success of an athletic event is measured by more than the final score. An efficient event management staff strives to provide a first-class event for the athletes, coaches and officials. Take pride in welcoming guests to the campus, community and athletic facility. The staff must believe in competing to win each game without sacrificing sportsmanship, service or hospitality. A service-oriented approach focuses on accommodating the needs of the home team, visitors, officials, fans and the many support staff required to operate the game.

The goal is to provide a competitive environment that allows the coaches and athletes to enter the athletic facility and be able to focus on what they do best: coach and compete. The teams and officials should be allowed to concentrate on the competition while the event staff plans, prepares and implements all management functions.

The event staff should be very concerned about maintaining a safe environment for the competitors, coaching staffs and officials.

Most importantly, the event staff should also be concerned about maintaining a safe environment for the competitors, coaching staffs and officials. To monitor crowd behavior and to ensure the safety of our guests, escort teams and officials to and from meeting rooms and assign a host to sit behind the visitors' bench. Make every effort to provide visitors with the same competitive environment the home team would appreciate having on the road. Do not turn up the heat to dehydrate the coaches and athletes; open the windows to create wind currents; or make the visiting team sit on benches while the home team players sit in cushy chairs. These things have been known to happen on the road! The game needs to remain on the court rather than off the court.

Successful event management is not difficult! It simply takes pre-planning, communication and a responsible staff with a service-oriented work ethic. Then, why have coaches walked into a facility and never known who was responsible for managing the event? Has service-oriented event management been a priority in the program? If a team is striving to be the best on the court, why not host a first-class event so an entire athletic program can be showcased as one of the best in the league or conference?

> Successful event management is not difficult! It simply takes pre-planning, communication and a responsible staff with a service-oriented work ethic.

As coaches, it is important to take some responsibility to make sure every team or official visiting the school is accommodated in a first-class manner. It is important to treat guests at home as a team would like to be treated on the road. Investing time and effort into home events may pay off on the next road trip. This does not mean the head coach should be the event manager; concentrate on coaching! However, since event management is a direct reflection on a program, playing a role in the selection of a responsible, service-oriented individual as the event manager is important. He/she may be a staff member in the department, a graduate as-

An effective event manager can be a staff member in the department, a graduate assistant, an assistant coach, a student coach or possibly a mature undergraduate student interested in pursuing a career in athletic management.

sistant, an assistant coach, a student coach or possibly a mature undergraduate student interested in pursuing a career in athletic administration. Once someone is assigned this responsibility, the coach or athletic director must take the time to evaluate the performance of the event manager and her/his staff. Since an event manager should know the sport and facility (and what coaches and athletes need), their feedback is an important element of hosting a first-class event. If the job is not getting done, set up a meeting with the administration or the person responsible for event management to discuss ways to improve the hosting of home events. Share ideas and then help with identifying ways to recruit a service oriented staff.

Service-oriented event management will help showcase a team as one of the more respected programs in the conference or league.

EVENT MANAGEMENT GUIDELINES
Philosophy - Run a First-Class Event

Establish a philosophy similar to the "better the ball" philosophy emphasized in volleyball. Just as the volleyball team is striving to make each contact of the ball better than the previous contact, work hard to make the management of each event better than the previous event. Set a goal to have the best event management in the conference or league. Take the opportunity to showcase the program.

ESTABLISH A SERVICE-ORIENTED STAFF

Plan, evaluate and make decisions with a service-oriented approach. The objective of event management is to accommodate the needs of everyone involved with the event.

HIRE A SERVICE-ORIENTED STAFF

Recruit and organize an event staff to accommodate or assist with the following: visiting teams, officials, security and ticket operations, promotional activities, game operations table, statistics crew, ball crew, athletic training and facility set-up and take-down. Take the time to recruit and train volunteers, student help or work groups in search of a fund raiser.

PRE-PLAN TO PREVENT NIGHTMARES

Take care of details during pre-planning. Be prepared, yet flexible. Outline specific areas of responsibility and distribute to event staff.

IDENTIFY ROLES AND RESPONSIBILITIES

Meet with the event staff before the season starts and review responsibilities. Emphasize professionalism and service. Then, meet on a consistent basis throughout the season to evaluate performance and make any necessary adjustments. Also, meet with security and ticket takers prior to each event to provide game instructions and to emphasize "Service With A Smile."

PROVIDE AN INFORMATIONAL PACKET TO THE VISITING TEAM

Communicate with the visiting team's head or assistant coach prior to the team's arrival. Mail campus, community, facility and game information at least two months prior to the season beginning. Include a time schedule for pre-game countdown, the type of game ball to be used, lockerroom and meeting room availability/assignment, parking permits, campus and facility maps, motel/restaurant information, medical emergency information, names and numbers for key athletic staff. Also provide a visitors travel information and practice request form to be completed and returned so you can more effectively plan for and meet their needs. If necessary, offer to assist with lodging/travel arrangements for either the officials or teams.

COMMUNICATE: CONFIRM PRACTICES ASAP

Confirm practice times in writing at least two weeks prior to the event. Make every effort to schedule practices in the game facility and at the time requested by the visitors.

BE PREPARED TO MAKE DECISIONS

No matter how well you plan, problems or changes will occur before or during an event. Do not panic! Be flexible, think before acting, prioritize if necessary and then make decisions based on the safety of those involved, NCAA and conference rules and your service-oriented philosophy.

IF YOU DELEGATE, BE SURE TO FOLLOW-UP

Make sure the event staff is following through with service-oriented event management philosophies and expectations.

MEET YOUR VISITORS AT THE FRONT DOOR AT THE SCHEDULED TIME

Meet the team and officials when they first enter the facility. Introduce yourself as the event manager and determine who on the coaching staff will be your contact person during the event. Provide a time schedule and escort the team to the lockerroom or meeting room. Offer your services! Do the same for the officials.

BE READY FOR YOUR VISITORS' ARRIVAL

Make sure the facility is set up, ball carts by the team benches and floor swept before the teams and officials enter the facility.

PROVIDE YOUR GUESTS A HOST OR ESCORT

Assign a host to each team and identify areas of responsibilities. Make

In athletics, it is important to be a good host when teams visit your campus. Providing a positive first impression is very important. Your cooperation and assistance in their trip planning will provide not only a great first impression, but a lasting one. The Golden Rule of "treating others as you would want to be treated" should be strictly adhered to when preparing for your guest's visit.

Before a visiting team sets foot on campus, there are many ways you can assist with their arrangements. An Athletic Service Directory which is updated and sent yearly to conference members and to other school that visit during the upcoming year can be very helpful. The directory contains the following:

- Staff Directory - names, titles, phone numbers, addresses, fax number, email address.
- Lodging - recommended local hotels, addresses, phone numbers, contact names, rates.
- Restaurants - local restaurants, addresses, phone numbers.
- Transportation - recommended charter companies and rental agencies, addresses, phone numbers, contact names.
- Medical Information - athletic training services, trainers' and physicians' names and phone numbers, hospital information.
- Maps and Directions - campus-area maps, directions to campus.
- Request for Services Form - to be completed by the visiting coach and returned to us; includes travel arrangement information, requests for practice, equipment, video, athletic training and laundry services.

(Masser, Joan. Playing the perfect host. *Coaching Volleyball*, August/September 1991, 30.)

sure visitors and officials have towels and water on the bench and towels/soap available in the lockerroom following the game. Recruiting volunteers to host the visiting team and officials is a key aspect of service-oriented event management and is the first step in making your visitors feel at home in your facility. This personal touch is the foundation for hosting a first-class event.

BE VISIBLE AND INVOLVED AT THE EVENT

During the event, the event manager should be visible and near courtside. Be within eye contact of the officials. Monitor crowd behavior, especially behind the team bench area. Confront a situation before it becomes a problem.

EVALUATE PERFORMANCE

Always ask the event staff what would make the event better and then request feedback from the coaching staff. If you are already doing all of the above, then take a look at how it is getting done. How could it be done better?

REMEMBER, SERVICE IS AN ATTITUDE

Coaches, take an interest in event management and take the time to make sure you and your institution are providing the athletes, officials and fans with a first-class event. Resources should not be a limiting factor. Service is an attitude, not a budget line item. Managing an event in a first-class manner is not expensive, but it does take time to organize, recruit and motivate support staff and student help. Utilize the following groups, which have been found to be efficient and cost effective:

Monitor crowd behavior, especially behind the team bench area. A good event manager should confront a situation before it becomes a potential problem.

1) *Volunteers from the community.* Individuals from service groups, senior citizen centers or youth groups are always looking for fund raisers, or more importantly, an identity with a college team. Since resources are limited, the least expensive way to staff an event is to hire a group and pay a minimum group rate. It is a win-win situation for everyone. The group makes a little money and develops an identity with the team and it gains a loyal following.

2) *Students in the sports management minor or major.* The undergraduate students work as team and officials' hosts for home events. They provide the teams and officials the extra attention they seldom receive on the road.

3) *Campus groups interested in fund raising "work" projects.* Use ROTC units, sports clubs, Fellowship of Christian Athletes and students in the university choir. Again, first-rate event management is service and service is an attitude. Attitude is cost-free and is easily attained if cultivated by the coach, administration and event manager. Once a ser-

vice-oriented attitude becomes a priority, there are a variety of ways to develop a professional event management staff within the resources of the program.

*Pam Bradetich is the former administrative assistant/events manager at Washington State University in Pullman, Wash.

Improving Your Team's Media Coverage

Improving Your Team's Media Coverage — Dan Dittmer

Volleyball matches do not get the same depth of treatment in most local newspapers as certain other sports. Basketball, softball, baseball and football are covered in detail with statistics and game descriptions. But rather than simply complain about this inequity, volleyball coaches can do something to obtain better coverage for their teams. One reason for poor volleyball coverage may be that few sportswriters have played the game—whereas many know other sports from the player's viewpoint. Not all of the blame for sparse coverage can be placed on reporters—some must rest on the shoulders of volleyball coaches. Coaches who want better coverage must educate reporters about the game.

Examine these two fictitious news write-ups. Which gives you a collection of statistics and which goes further to tell a story? Which is more typical of the coverage you get?

If a player is mobbed by reporters after a big kill in an important game, he/she will be more at ease if you have prepared him/her for the interview process and what reporters are looking for.

- *West Olympic Wins in Three*

The West Olympic Aces defeated the East Olympic Tigers, 17-15, 12-15, 17-15, to win the Jefferson County championship last night at East Olympic High. The Aces and Tigers begin district action next week at West Olympic High.

Topping the Aces were Tracy North with 15 kills, Vanessa Lapland with 12 and Angela Jones with 11. Kim Rogers had a great night passing the ball for the Aces, according to coach Danielle Price.

- *West Olympic Rallies to Beat East*

The West Olympic Aces rallied from a 13-6 third-game deficit to cap a 17-15, 12-15, 17-15 victory over the East Olympic Tigers last night at East Olympic High. The win gave the Aces, who host the Tigers in district action next week, the Jefferson County championship.

In the final game, Vanessa Lapland started the Aces' comeback with four consecutive aces that cut the Tigers' lead to three points. Following a Tiger time-out, West Olympic's Kim Rogers dug out a spike and passed to setter Cathy Beal, who set Angela Jones for another point. A Tiger error was followed by another Rogers-Beal-Jones combination to tie the score at 13. [And the article continues, describing the winning points.]

Unfortunately, most volleyball results read like the first example. Though both stories give the reader the five W's of reporting (who, what, when, where, why), the second supplies more detail. In the first example, the coach supplied the reporter only with statistics — not that it is wrong, it is just not enough. (But at least it gets the players' names — though usually only the hitters—into the paper.)

Coaches seem naturally inclined to supply only statistics—that is part of the problem. Also, most coaches work with reporters unfamiliar with power volleyball. Some reporters complain that volleyball does not have sustained long drives, innings where teams score crucial runs or fourth-

If your volleyball match does not have much media coverage, get the information to the media yourself. Help reporters become more knowledgeable about volleyball by discussing it with them.

quarter rallies. But it does have kills, digs, roofing blocks and great rallies for coaches to tell about. This point is illustrated in the second write-up. One would almost expect such a story to be about some other sport than volleyball!

Most newspaper reports of a school's matches describe detail beyond mere statistics. To ensure this practice, keep a running score data sheet of matches to report something more than numbers. Tally kills for points and side-outs, important turning points in a game or match, digs, blocks, passes, set assists and much more (see Figure 1). The assistant coach, usually with the help of a player on the bench, can collect the raw data. From the sheets, construct the details to be provided to the newspaper.

From the sample sheet, notice that a close 7-6 game was broken open with four straight points by Team A. Player 10 (always supply full names to the press) scored three aces and No. 8 got a tip kill with a set assist to No. 9. The remaining points are as easily delineated.

In creating the running data score sheet, our first challenge was coming up with the codes. For example, ESL is error—serve long; EKN is error—kill in net; K is kill; and so on. Improvise and invent new symbols as needed (such as ME—mental error). With time and experience, using the running score data sheet can become second nature to staff and players.

For a year or two reporters continued to take only statistics from us when we called our game results into the papers. Gradually, though, change has taken place and we like to think we are continuing to educate our local reporters about volleyball. Now local sportswriters are more than willing to publish articles about our team like the earlier second example. Even when we lose a match we usually get more print than the winner! When we call in our results we are asked for statistics and details. We provide the reporters with more information than they can use.

Reporters appreciate the greater detail and players enjoy reading the story more than a report that "Jane Stevens had three kills and Julie Cone had two with three aces as East beat West, 15-8."

We encourage coaches to consider using the running score data sheet to give more than just numbers to their local papers. Players deserve better coverage and we can help them get it.

Newspaper accounts of baseball, softball, basketball and football almost always include more than statistics. So should volleyball.

Dan Dittmer is the former head girls' volleyball coach at Chimacum High School (Chimacum, Wash.).

Ten Tips to Improve Media Relations

1. Be honest. Do not use the media to issue a false injury report or to make other statements that are not true solely to "psych" an opponent. You do not want to lose your credibility.
2. Provide parking at matches for reporters and give them working space in the gym.
3. If reporters do not cover a match, get the information to the media yourself. Know the preferred times to call. Always return phone calls. Be accessible.
4. Help reporters become more knowledgeable about volleyball by discussing it with them. Reporters are always looking for a good human interest story. If you know of a possibility (maybe your setter is also a nationally known pianist or one of your players has overcome a major obstacle to achieving success on the court), let the media know.
5. Communicate the kind of publicity your team needs. At least at the high school level, reporters may be willing to work with you on this.
6. Send out a fact sheet, including an accurate roster of names, vital statistics and schedules.
7. Correct mistakes. If you notice an error in print, inform the paper. Hint: When spelling a name over the phone, emphasize easily misunderstood letters, e.g., "S as in Susan," or "F as in Frank."
8. Be friendly and cooperative. Talking to the media after a loss can be difficult, but it is a professional necessity. Remember, when talking to a reporter, you are talking to the public.
9. Be patient about results. Often there are more stories to cover than space will allow. Your persistence will show the media you care and they will respond.
10. Teach players how to deal with the media. If a player is mobbed by reporters after a big kill in an important game, he/she will be more at ease if you have prepared him/her for the interview process and what reporters are looking for.

Figure 1
Sample Running Score Data Sheet

A—Assist
K—Kill
Blk—Block
T—Tip kill
EP—Error on pass
FF—Foot fault
EN—Error net

ES—Service error
EK—Attack error
EB—Blocking error
ET—Tip error
EST—Error on set
TO—Time out

Team _____
Site _____
Date _____
Game _____

(For errors, can indicate <u>N</u>et, <u>L</u>ong, or <u>O</u>ut left or right)

Points A	B	Side-outs A	B	Running score	Points A	B	Side-outs A	B	Running score
7/9A 12K				1-0	10EKL				7-4
		10EKL			7EP				7-5
8EKN				1-1	9 EB out				7-6
			3ESN					1ENET	
		9ESL					12EKL		7-6
	1A 6K			1-2				6EKL	
		10BLK KILL			10ACE				8-6
		12EP LIFT		2-2	10ACE				9-6
8UTK				3-2	9A 8TK				10-6
		11-K			10ACE				11-6
	5/1A			3-3			12EKL		
		12EKL			12ACE				11-7
7UK				4-3			12ESN		
		12ESL			12ACE				12-7
		3EKN					12ESN		
7/9A 8TK				5-3 5-3			9/7A 8K		
11A 8K				6-3	8EN				13-7
		7ESL					5A 3K		
ME(OOPS)				6-4			11A		13-8
		9A 8TK					12/7A 11K		
7A				7-4	8ACE				14-8
		8ESN			12/9A 10K				15-8
		14ESN							

Best of Coaching Volleyball: Improving Your Team's Media Coverage

Increasing Your Volleyball Program's Income

Increasing Your Volleyball Program's Income

DARLENE KLUKA, PH.D.

With escalating budgetary constraints on interscholastic and intercollegiate sport programs, additional income to volleyball programs has become increasingly important in recent years. To continue enhancing your volleyball program, you may need to generate revenue from alternative sources. Creative thought and fundraising are frequently critical to a program's maintenance and growth.

IDEAS

Community Events. Develop an exhibit of your volleyball program for local libraries, open houses, recognition dinners and health fairs. The exhibit might include a slide presentation, videos of local team matches, handouts or rules, volleyball techniques and a season schedule.

Educational Support. You and your staff can provide training for novice volleyball coaches, officials and players through volleyball workshops or clinics where participants pay a clinic fee.

PSAs. Provide local media with public service announcements for upcoming matches and events to increase your community visibility.

Sponsorships. Seek grants from local community leaders, corporations and the Women's Sports Foundation. Grants and sponsorships could be used for a volleyball player development fund to assist players attending camps or clinics.

Publishing. With the advent and availability of desktop publishing, booklets on volleyball techniques, newsletters about volleyball and directories of volleyball supporters in the community can be created relatively easily and sold fairly inexpensively. Videotape of previous matches or skill techniques can also be manufactured for rental. Use of the Internet to provide publishable information to volleyball supporters can be easily made available, as well.

Products. Apparel (T-shirts, jackets, ties, sunglasses), pens, mugs, paperweights, license plate holders, shoe laces, keychains and other kinds of advertising specialties can be imprinted with your volleyball program's logo and sold to enthusiasts.

Auctions. Bring in a well-known volleyball player to host an auction of old uniforms, equipment, autographed volleyballs and so on. Urge your supporters and alumni to donate equipment and volleyball-related articles.

Wish List. Develop a list of desired equipment for your program and publicize it through a newsletter to community businesses who support you.

Long-term Business Relationships. Establish long-term relationships with local businesses for three- to five-year projects that are mutually beneficial. For example, establish an annual "ABC Company Volleyball Player of the Year

A carefully planned exhibit can provide the community with a closer look at your volleyball program and perhaps increase ticket sales and/or sponsorship opportunities.

The following is a list of qualities needed to enhance fund raising effectiveness:

- **Faith:** A person must possess strong convictions for the program and/or institution for which they are striving to improve.
- **Intuition:** Questions such as, "Who is the right person to approach a particular propsect?" must be asked.
- **Creativity:** Allow yourself to look beyond the ordinary.
- **Confidence:** If you know what you are selling and believe in it, then confidence will follow.
- **Clarity:** Have an understanding of where you are going and how to get there.
- **Commitment:** Have strong convictions toward the things that you are doing.
- **Enthusiasm:** Bring life to concepts with which we wish to create.
- **Perseverance:** It can take years to build a successful program or organization.
- **Adaptability:** Successful leaders of successful organizations embrace change, even look forward to it.
- **Compassion:** Show the people from whom you are soliciting funds that you are truly interested in them.
- **Integrity:** Do what you say you are going to do.
- **Gratitude:** Acknowledge every gift.

(Allen, Ed. Fund raising a key to success. *Coaching Volleyball*, April/May 1996, 18-19.)

> You and your staff can provide training for novice volleyball coaches, officials and players through volleyball workshops or clinics where participants pay a clinic fee.

Award." This could increase ticket sales for your annual banquet while improving patronage for the sponsor.

Rentals. Rent volleyball equipment to local groups. Designate part of the profit for replacement of equipment when necessary.

Ad Sales. Sell advertising space in your volleyball programs (which are sold at your matches). Sell advertising space in other sport programs and get a percentage returned to your program.

SUMMARY

The future of your volleyball program rests in your hands. Through innovative generation of additional income, your program will be provided with the nutrients necessary to take root, blossom and bloom for years to come.

Darlene Kluka, Ph.D., is the coordinator of Graduate Studies at the University of Central Oklahoma and serves on the USA Volleyball Sports Medicine and Performance Committee and the *Coaching Volleyball* Editorial Board.

Section VI: Statistics

The Statistics Crew: Vital to Your Program

The Statistics Crew: Vital to Your Program

GRANT BURGER

Though most coaches thrive on statistics, compiling them can be an aggravating chore. From selecting a stat crew to making sure they understand how to keep the records, coaches often find this task frustrating.

From a different perspective, the American Volleyball Coaches Association also shares in the frustration. The AVCA staff, which documented NCAA Division I weekly national statistics from 1984-93, has continually noticed two major problems: inaccuracy and inconsistency.

Pinpointing the cause of these problems is not easy. Common snafus include statistical interpretations and a high turnover rate of stat workers. Indeed, proper record keeping is a process that begins with dedicated people—the stat crew.

A knowledgeable statistics crew is very important to a coach, as effective statistics can save a coach a number of headaches after a match.

FORMING A DEPENDABLE STATISTICS CREW

The primary key to forming a successful stat crew is finding responsible, dependable people. If they already know volleyball, that is all the better. But do not limit yourself. Often former athletes or statisticians from other sports can make the transition with instruction.

The secondary key is having the same people work together at every match. Whether you are using a two-, three- or four-person system, this practice works in your favor. Consistency is paramount to accurate statistics.

> The primary key to forming a successful stat crew is finding responsible, dependable people. If they already know volleyball, that is all the better. But do not limit yourself. Often former athletes or statisticians from other sports can make the transition with instruction.

If you are a collegiate coach with a knowledgeable sports information director, you probably will not be heading up a statistics crew. But it is best to check with your SID to make sure everything is in order.

TEACHING THE GAME

"What is an overlap?"

"Is a tip the same thing as an attack?"

You have undoubtedly heard many such questions if you have ever accepted the challenge of teaching new volleyball statisticians. Several simple steps can ensure your statistics crew knows the basics and can, in the process, save you headaches. (First, have your crew read the *National Volleyball Statistics Manual* and watch the video; then stat a practice or scrimmage before the first home match.)

A good exercise is to chart a videotaped match. This exposes the crew to on-court situations they will see time and again. If someone has a question you can back up and watch the play again. You can even run plays in slow motion to emphasize certain points. If you do not have much footage, have your manager videotape a scrimmage.

Through this exercise your new stat crew members will become more comfortable with their responsibility, and experienced members should find the refresher useful.

SELECTING YOUR STAT SYSTEM

After determining and orienting your statistics crew, you need to identify the best system to use.

If you are keeping statistics for both your team and your opponent (as often happens in intercollegiate competition), these systems will work:

• Four-person: By far the most accurate system. Two people are assigned to each team. One person calls court action to the partner, who records the information on paper. Each two-person team is responsible only for their assigned team.

Three-person: In this system one person calls the action for both teams. The caller is flanked by the two recorders who document the stats of their assigned teams. The most knowledgeable person should call the action. The system works best if the three sit in the bleachers. This provides greater court visibility and cuts down on the chance of being blocked by an official.

An efficient computer statistics program can help your crew to provide accurate stats after a match.

• Two-person: In this system, one person documents the action for each team. If you have two very knowledgeable people this system can work fine, especially if they concentrate on the positive key stats (kills, blocks, aces). However, with new people this system can be tough and prone to errors.

If you are responsible for just your own team, modifications of the same basic systems can be followed:

• Four-person. One pair calls and documents attacking and setting categories while the other pair calls and documents passing, defense, serving, and blocking.

• Three-person. Category assignments are the same for recorders but there is only one caller.

• Two-person. This system has two options. One person can call while the other person charts or one can watch and chart attacking and setting while the other handles passing, defense, serving and blocking.

The key ingredient to a dependable stat crew is commitment. Make them feel like part of the team, a vital component in your season adventure. In time, you will have a stat crew that is not only dependable, but efficient and accurate.

Grant Burger is the former director of sports information for the American Volleyball Coaches Association.

A Simple Statistical System for High School Volleyball

A Simple Statistical System for High School Volleyball

SID FELDMAN

Collecting data during a volleyball match is the most difficult part of developing a valid analysis of individual match performance. I have developed the system described here to make gathering statistics for high school teams easier.

This statistics system can be used at all levels of competition and has been placed into a computer format by Rod Schall (assistant men's volleyball coach) at Graceland College in Lamoni, Iowa. Schall's sophisticated system can be used for either the NCAA form or high school and provides good information. Although computer analysis results in more efficient information retrieval at the end of the match, the handwritten approach I describe is just as easy to use.

As statisticians and coaches know, collecting data during a volleyball match is the most difficult part of developing a valid analysis of individual match performance.

The categories have been changed from the standard NCAA box score because high schools require less information about blocking and more about serve and serve receive. The passing categories include passes to the setter, passes handled by someone other than the setter and aces (not touched by more than one player). In addition, several percentage categories have been added to demonstrate the effectiveness of the server.

Unlike the NCAA form, this system does not require that the data be transposed to a match box score. The raw data sheet can be passed among the participants since shared team statistical data is unnecessary at the high school level.

This system requires two individuals—typically two junior varsity players. One calls every touch on a ball while the other records the touches with a slash mark, thus making the results available immediately following the match.

USING THE SYSTEM

Figure 1 is an example of the raw data sheet. Figure 2 is a sample to be used in conjunction with the following explanation. List players numerically, except for the setters, who should be listed in the two bottom rows.

Serve receive

1. Draw a slash mark (/) in the Serve Receive box every time a player attempts to receive a serve. Leave the slash mark if the pass goes to the setter.

2. Change the slash to an X if the pass goes off target and is saved by someone other than the setter.

3. Change the slash to an E if the ball hits the ground without being touched. Assign the E to the player standing closest to the ball when it hits the ground. An E is also assigned to a player if the initial serve receive is touched but is never touched by a second player. The E represents an error and refers to the receiver being aced.

•At the end of the match: total the number of slash marks and place in

FIGURE 1

# Name	GP	Serve Receive				Attack				Defense		Serving (SEf=SA-%SE)				
		G=	B=	U=	%G=G/TA	K=	E=	TA=	%=K-E/TA	Digs	Blocks	SA=	SE=	TA=	S.Ef=	SA%
Setter						A=	TA=		%=A/TA=							
Setter						A=	TA=		%=A/TA=							

FIGURE 2

# Name	GP	Serve Receive				Attack				Defense		Serving (SEf=SA-%SE)				
		G=	B=	U=	%G=G/TA	K=	E=	TA=	%=K-E/TA	Digs	Blocks	SA=	SE=	TA=	S.Ef=	SA%
3 Liz Bauer	2 //	4 //XEE//XEX	3	3	400	5 //KKKEE//KK	2	10	300	4 ////	3 ///	2 //AAE//	1	7	1.5	
11 Mary Low	1 /															
9 Kate Tebo	2 //															
Setter 7 Hanes	3 ///	1 /	0	0	1.0	A=4 ///AAA///A	TA=10		%=A/TA=.40 KE/K	1 /////	1 4 .25 //////////	7 E///A//	12	1	3	.5

the Good (G) box.

• Total the number of X's and place in the Bad (B) box.

• Total the number of E's and place in the Ugly! (U) box.

• Total the number of receives and divide by the number of good receives; write this percentage in the %G box.

ATTACK

1. Place a slash mark in the Attack box every time a player attempts to send the ball across the net. Leave the slash mark if the ball is dug by the opposing team (see definition of dig below).

2. Change the slash to a K if the attack results in an immediate point or side-out. At the end of the match: total the number of K's and write the total in the Kill box. Total the number of E's and write the total in the Error box.

Total the number of /'s. Add this number, the total errors and the total

Feldman's statistical system can be used at all levels of competition and does not require a large number of statisticians.

Photo: Dan Houser

kills; place the result in the Total Attempts (TA) box. Subtract errors from kills; then divide by total attempts and place this percentage in the % box.

DIGS

Place a slash in the digs column only when the ball is successfully dug. A dig is awarded to a player whenever a player passes the ball which has been attacked by the opposition. Digs are only given when players receive an attacked ball and it is kept in play.

BLOCKS

Place a slash in the blocks column only when a successful block has occurred (one which results in an immediate side-out or point.) Note: If more than one player is involved in the block, then all players receive credit for the block, even when you can identify the specific blocker who actually touched the ball.

SERVING

Record a slash mark in the Serves column every time a player serves the ball. Leave the slash mark if the play continues. Change the slash to an A if the server aced the opposing team. (See the definition under "Serve Receive" to determine if an ace has occurred.) Change the slash to an E if a service error occurs (e.g., served in net).

AT THE END OF THE MATCH

- Total the number of A's and record in the Service Ace (SA) box.
- Total the number of E's and place the total in the Service Error (SE) box.
- Total the number of slash marks. Add this to the total of aces and errors and place the result in the Total Attempts (TA) box.
- Subtract half the number of service errors from the service aces (SA); record the number in the Service Efficiency (S.Ef) box.
- Divide service aces by total attempts to determine percentage of ace serves.

SETTING (FOR SETTERS ONLY)

Place a slash in the setter's box every time a setter touches a second ball. Change the slash to an A if the set results in an assist. An assist is any pass that is turned into a kill on the next touch.

AT THE END OF THE MATCH

- Total the number of A's and record in the Assist (A) box. Total the number of slash marks.
- Add to the number of assists and record this amount in the Total Attempts box.
- Divide the assists by the total attempts and place this percentage in the % box.

*Sid Feldman is the former head women's volleyball coach at the University of Georgia in Athens, Ga.

Recording Volleyball Statistics Easily: The Schroeder System
Lois Mueller

The importance of accurate volleyball statistics cannot be over-emphasized. They are needed for coaching decisions, match and season evaluations, individual and team rankings and player honors. Yet, recording accurate volleyball statistics can be a very difficult task.

There are a number of factors which contribute to the difficulty of recording statistics. First, some of the moves requiring statistical data occur in rapid succession, such as the set and the attack. Second, certain statistics are defined by what occurs afterward. An assist cannot be credited until the result of the attack is known. In these cases, the statistician must remember the players involved while observing the attack, then record both occurrences. Third, keeping statistics requires subjective judgments which must be made quickly and consistently. The difference between an ace for one server and a passing error for an opposing receiver can be very difficult to decipher.

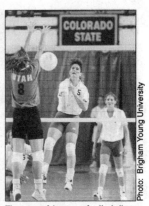
The nature of the game of volleyball makes it difficult to keep accurate stats.

THE PROBLEM

Numerous methods of recording match data have been tried in an attempt to keep accurate and consistent volleyball statistics. (Many programs have sufficient funding for courtside computer programs or the necessary crews to collect statistical data; however, a number of high school or smaller college programs are not afforded that luxury.) One possible tack to help overcome this problem is to have one or more persons tally all occurrences on a stat sheet as they occur in each game. A typical stat sheet lists each statistical category in a column across the top of the form while players' names and/or numbers are listed in rows down the left margin. The columns are subdivided into positive and negative outcomes of each statistic, as well as occurrences (e.g., serving attempts, aces and errors).

The difficulty of using this method stems from the time required to find the correct row and column in which to record the tally. The correct player row must first be located and then the statistician must move across the row until arriving at the appropriate stat column to record the tally

> Numerous methods of recording match data have been tried in an attempt to keep accurate and consistent volleyball statistics. (Many programs have sufficient funding for courtside computer programs or the necessary crews to collect statistical data; however, a number of high school or smaller college programs are not afforded that luxury.

or vice versa. While doing this searching and recording, subsequent play is often missed. Using more than one statistician can make this method workable, if responsibilities are wisely divided and procedures are clearly understood. However, since skilled statisticians are difficult to find and teams must often limit traveling squads, choosing a method of keeping statistics requiring two or more people may not be possible.

A second method of keeping volleyball statistics requires the statistician to do a verbal play-by-play into a tape recorder. For example, "No. 15 passes serve; No. 3 sets; No. 12 attacks for the kill; assist to No. 3." This enables the statistician to keep his/her eyes on the court while talking into the recorder. Comments regarding assists and other outcome-related information can be added as play progresses. After the match, the

According to Mueller, the Schroeder System can turn a difficult and problematic procedure into a relatively easy task.

tape is transcribed onto a stat sheet.

While this method solves many of the problems encountered in the first method, it is extremely time-consuming. Transcribing the tape—even without stopping it to record tallies—involves nearly the same amount of time as the match consumed...hours. If the tape must be stopped and restarted while transcribing, even more time is involved. It is difficult to find a statistician who is willing to devote that amount of time. If more than one person is used (e.g., one person records the play-by-play while a second person transcribes the tape or different people cover different matches), inconsistent judgments and unclear interpretation can result.

A POSSIBLE SOLUTION

After struggling with these inefficient methods for many seasons, an alternative was developed. This system will be referred to as the Schroeder System, since it was developed by Susan Schroeder, the Concordia University volleyball statistician. The Schroeder System involves a stat sheet with columns for each major category similar to the first method described (see Figure 1). However, no player rows are necessary and only the basic statistical occurrence needs a column; no columns are needed for positive or negative outcomes.

As the game progresses, the statistician simply records the player's number anywhere in the appropriate column. This can be done with little attention to the chart since it is not necessary to find a specific row or place in the column. If an error is involved, the number is circled. If a positive result occurs such as an ace or kill, an asterisk is placed beside the number. This method enables one person to keep accurate statistics without spending numerous hours transcribing tapes. Since it is not necessary to locate rows for specific players or columns for positive or negative results, recording statistics is greatly simplified and the statistician is able to keep his/her eyes on the court and not on the clipboard. Other indicators can be used rather than the circle and the asterisk, if the statistician desires. After the match is completed, the stat sheets can be used to compute totals and percentages just as one would do with the tally stat sheet described in method one.

To simplify the post-match computations, it is recommended that the stat sheets be analyzed twice. The first time, only those numbers without circles or asterisks are crossed out, while a slash is placed through the circled and starred numbers. Then, on the second pass, the slashed numbers are recorded and totally crossed out. For example:

FIGURE 1

Serves	Serve Reception	Assists	Attacks	Digs	BS	BA	BHE	Other

prior to review
      15 5 ③ 12
       2 12* 5 11
after first analysis/review
      1̶5̶ 5̶ ③ 1̶2̶
       2̶ 1̶2̶* 5̶ 1̶1̶
after second analysis/review
      1̶5̶ 5̶ ⊗ 1̶2̶
       2̶ 1̶2̶ 5̶ 1̶1̶

SUMMARY

The ease of the Schroeder System is very functional. It can turn a difficult and problematic procedure into a relatively easy task. Using the Schroeder System allows the coach to concentrate on coaching, knowing that accurate statistics are being recorded.

*Lois Mueller is a former associate professor and head women's volleyball coach at Concordia University (Mequon, Wis.).

Chart a Path to Success With the Total Performance Chart

Chart a Path to Success With the Total Performance Chart

BRETT MILLS AND MICK MACK

As coaches, we are often asked by our players, "How did I play, coach?" Typically, our response is in vague, general terms like: "Great, really well or you were a little off tonight." Although our intent is to reinforce positively and motivate, we are giving non-specific information that is of little or no use to a player in an evaluative sense. Thus, a great opportunity to teach is lost. The Total Performance Chart described below enables coaches to provide specific feedback to their players, enhance a player's self-concept and enhance overall team cohesion.

TOTAL PERFORMANCE CHART

Providing specific knowledge of performance has been found to facilitate the learning of motor performance skills (Wallace and Hagler, 1979). Subjects who were provided specific information regarding their performances showed significantly higher levels of improvement when compared with subjects not receiving specific feedback. When provided descriptive and objective feedback, athletes are able to use this information to evaluate and learn from past performances. Additionally, providing feedback which holds each athlete personally accountable for his/her actions is one of the primary methods of combating social loafing. Social loafing is the notion that a player can get by with less than an all-out effort because of the presence of teammates (Cox, 1994). This explains why the sum total of the parts is often less than the sum of the individual parts. Holding each person accountable by evaluating individual performance has been found to be an effective method of reducing the negative effects of social loafing (Williams, Harkins and Latane, 1981). The Total Performance Chart (TPC) can be used for this purpose. Therefore, the TPC is able to provide the necessary feedback to facilitate learning and to reduce social loafing effects.

Providing specific knowledge of performance has been found to facilitate the learning of motor performance skills. Players no longer have to have their athletic abilities measured in vague, general terms.

As mentioned, the TPC was developed to provide informative feedback on player performances. It is an objective rating system that gives credit to the players who played the most complete game, not just the setters or big hitters. Basically, the chart awards plus points for assists, digs, blocks, kills and successful serves. Minus points are given for kill errors and missed serves.

The various skills have been weighted in an attempt to reflect their importance to the team. Specifically, two points are awarded for kills and serving aces. One point is awarded for kill attempts, assists, digs, blocks and successful serves. Conversely, two points are subtracted for a kill error or missed serve. All of these statistics can be obtained from the game stats sheet kept by most high school or college teams.

The formula used to tabulate each person's TPC score is then multiplied by the kill efficiency ratio. (The kill efficiency ratio is kills minus errors divided by attempts.) The result should be rounded off to the nearest whole number. This number is then added to successful serves (+1), aces (+2), missed serves (-2), digs (+1), assists (+1) and blocks (+1). Doing these calculations can result in either a positive or negative TPC rating (Figure 1).

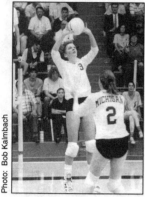

The athlete often associates the outcome of the event (win/loss) with his/her feelings of personal worth and value as a human being.

However, because not all matches involve the same number of games and because not all players participate in every game, these ratings can vary and might not give a true reading of performance. Therefore, the resultant TPC rating must sometimes be adjusted. In matches involving three games or in which the player participated in three games, no adjustments are needed. In matches involving a number of games other than three, an adjustment must be made. The adjustment is made by dividing the TPC rating by the number of games actually played. (This will probably vary by players, also.) Multiply this number by three to obtain the final TPC rating. This rating can now be compared with other performances on an equal basis. Players who might have actually played in fewer games can be compared to those who played in all of the games and vice versa because all statistics and ratings assume that three games were played (Figure 1).

Players who were provided specific information regarding their performances showed significantly higher levels of improvement when compared to those not receiving feedback.

FIGURE 1

	KILLS				ASSISTS	SERVING			DIGS	BLOCKS	GAMES
	KILLS	ERRORS	ATTEMPTS	EFFICIENCY		SUCCESS	ATTEMPTS	ACE			
Player A	11	1	19	.526	4	8	8	1	9	1	3
Player B	5	1	7	.571	0	1	2	0	1	3	4

(Kills - Errors + Attempts) X Efficiency Ratio
Player A (22-2 + 19) X .526 = 20.5 (rounded to 21)

Results + Assists + Success - Serve Errors + Aces + Digs + Blocks
21 + 4+ 8 - 0 + 2 + 9 + 1 = 45
Three games played so no adjustment is needed. TPC Rating = 45.

Player B (10 - 2 + 7) X 671 = 8.6 (rounded to 9)
9 + 0 + 1 - 2 + 0 + 1 + 3 = 12
Four games played so an adjustment is needed: (12/4) X 3 = TP C
3 X 3 = 9 TPC Rating

> Players who were provided specific information regarding their performances showed significantly higher levels of improvement when compared to those not receiving feedback.

TPC APPLIED TO SELF-CONCEPT

As coaches, we tend to emphasize how important the outcome of a certain match or competition is to the team, to us as coaches and to the players themselves. Unfortunately, the athlete often associates the outcome of the event (win/loss) with his/her feelings of personal worth and value as a human being (i.e., self-concept). This process can be very detrimental to an athlete's self-concept because there is often only one of two conclusions: winner or loser. With the TPC, an athlete is able to judge personal overall performance more specifically without regard to the team's win or loss record and as a result, enhance individual self-concept.

TPC APPLIED TO TEAM COHESION AND GOAL SETTING

An important aspect of all goal setting programs is the setting of both short- and long-term goals. For example, the short-term goal might be to win the upcoming tournament while the long-term goal is to reach the state tournament. Again, the outcome of these goals is often subjected to one of two conclusions: winner or loser. With the TPC, individuals and teams can set more specific short-term goals, i.e., by the fifth match of the season, everyone will increase their TPC score by two points. This goal is specific, obtainable and measurable. An additional benefit is that it is more precise when evaluating performance toward achieving that goal.

The use of the TPC can also enhance team cohesion because it enables each player to see individual contributions to the team as a whole. If a player only plays a portion of each game, they may have a similar TPC score as a player who plays the entire game. The player who only plays a few minutes can get a better sense of how they contribute to the team as a whole and as a result, may enhance the overall cohesion of the team.

REFERENCE RATINGS

In order to provide a general frame of reference, the actual TPC statistics for the entire 1993 season of a successful high school volleyball team will be presented. For the 16 matches involving 11 varsity players, individual TPC ratings ranged from -3 to 91. The team's primary setter had the highest average (52) with match scores ranging from 18 to 91. Both she and the team's best outside hitter were unanimous first-team all-conference selections. The all-conference outside hitter averaged 41 points, with a range of 12 to 54. The other starters had averages between six and 32, while non-starters had averages between four and 11.

SUMMARY

In summary, the Total Performance Chart is an objective rating system that provides feedback on player performance. It awards positive points for good plays and negative points for mistakes. The calculations are adjusted so that all performances can be compared on an equal basis. However, the most beneficial aspect of the TPC is that it provides descriptive, objective feedback which facilitates learning, reduces the negative effects of social loafing, improves self-concept and enhances team cohesion.

REFERENCES

Cox, R.H. (1994). *Sport Psychology: Concepts and Applications*, 3rd ed. Dubuque, IA: Wm. C. Brown Communications.

Wallace, S.A., Hagler, R.W. (1979). Knowledge of performance and the learning of a closed motor skill. *Research Quarterly, 50,* 205-271.

Williams, K., Harkins, S.G. Latane, B. (1981). Identifiability as a deterrent to social loafing: two cheering experiments. *Journal of Personality and Social Psychology, 40,* 303-311.

Brett Mills is the director of research at the U.S. Sports Academy in Daphne, Ala. Mick Mack is a sport psychology instructor at the University of Northern Iowa (Cedar Falls, Iowa).

There is some support that indicates that social loafing may be more prevalent in sport teams comprised of female athletes (Everett, et. al., 1992). This study was comprised of swimmers in the relay event and indicated, "Females who experienced relatively low cohesion were more likely to demonstrate the social loafing effect when performing..." (Everett, et. al., 1992). Conversely, those female athletes who experienced high task cohesion were less likely to exhibit the social loafing effect.

Additionally, the Everett, Smith and Williams (1992) study indicated, "...females seemed more likely to help individuals with whom they had close, long-term relationships." This study would suggest that quality sport performance would be more closely related to the quality of interpersonal relationships with female athletes than male athletes. "If this is true, psychological interventions designed to promote and enhance relationships among team members such as team building may be more beneficial for female athletes than males" (Everett, et. al., 1992).

(Eide, Carolyn. Social loafing and volleyball. *Coaching Volleyball*, October/November 1995, 31.)

What is the AVCA?

The mission of the American Volleyball Coaches Association is to advance the development of the sport of volleyball by providing coaches with educational programs, a forum for opinion exchange and recognition opportunities. Member participation is vital to the association accomplishing this mission.

The following principles guide the AVCA in the attainment of its goals: To maintain a membership group representative of all levels of competition; to promote the game of volleyball within the general philosophical framework of education; to encourage participation within the highest standards of competition; and to develop greater interest, understanding and support of the sport.

HISTORY OF THE AVCA

In 1981, the AVCA was incorporated as a private non-profit 501-(c)-3 educational corporation. The original Board of Directors consisted of eight NCAA Division I collegiate coaches. A part-time executive director administered the programs.

As the AVCA began to grow and diversify, a full-time executive director was hired in July 1983. An associate director was hired in April 1986 and an administrative assistant in September 1988.

In August 1992, the association moved from San Mateo, Calif., to Colorado Springs, Colo. The staff has increased to the following positions: executive director, director of membership services, assistant director of membership services, director of sports information, director of publishing, sports information assistant and part-time accountant. In addition, the association employs interns and other part-time people.

In 1986, the Board was increased to 13 members, and in 1987 and 1989, the Board was increased to enfranchise first the high school and then the junior communities.

Membership increased steadily from 1981 through 1987 (about 150 new members per year), followed by a 106 percent boom in 1988. Since 1986, high school membership has more than tripled. High school coaches from 46 states and the District of Columbia are members. At the collegiate level, all major NCAA conferences are represented and membership among the club coaches has risen dramatically.

The original members of the AVCA were all intercollegiate coaches who banned together to unite this particular coaching body. They have been the backbone of the association's existence and a united voice determining volleyball's future.

Perhaps the most significant decision was made at the San Francisco convention in 1986, however, when the membership recognized the growing and developing high school and club communities. The name of the association was changed to reflect these growing constituencies. From the original Collegiate Volleyball Coaches Association, the American Volleyball Coaches Association was born with the intent of responding to and serving all volleyball coaches.

SERVICE FUNCTIONS

The AVCA services its members through more varied functions than almost any other coaches' organization. The AVCA only involves itself with activities that best exemplify the image of amateur athletics. Its ultimate mission is to enhance the image and increase awareness for the sport of volleyball. Listed below are summaries of just some of the many AVCA activities:

1. The AVCA serves as the main liaison between its members and the NCAA for sport legislation. This role is vital in that the AVCA communicates members' beliefs and opinions on issues affecting volleyball and its participants.

2. The AVCA prepares, edits and distributes 12 monthly newsletters and six professional journals to all of its members. Associate members receive 12 news-

letters/drill bulletins that deal with issues affecting high school and juniors coaches. College members receive a weekly publication during the season that covers the ongoing results and activities of teams around the country.

    3. The AVCA orchestrates a series of awards programs which recognize the competitive efforts of more than 325 student-athletes and coaches. These programs include acknowledging athletes at the regional/district levels, as well as on the national level. These programs are for all Division levels and are as listed:

- For NCAA Division I
  - Eight (8) All-District Teams - 1st and 2nd: 12 members each
- For NCAA Division II
  - Eight (8) All-Region Teams - 1st and 2nd: 12 members each
- For NCAA Division III
  - Eight (8) All-Region Teams - 1st and 2nd: 12 members each
- For NCAA Divisions I, II, III, NAIA & Junior College/Community College:
  - All-America Teams - 24 recipients each
  - National "Player of the Year" - 5 recipients
  - Coaches "Victory Club" Award
  - National "Coach of the Year" - 5 recipients
  - Region "Coach of the Year "- 8 (Div II), 8 (Div III), 9 (NAIA), 8 (JC/CC)
  - District "Coach of the Year" - 8 (Div I)
- For Men
  - All-America Teams - 18 recipients
  - National "Player of the Year"
  - Coaches "Victory Club" Award
  - National "Coach of the Year"

    4. The AVCA organizes and conducts an annual convention and clinic for all its membership in conjunction with the NCAA Division I Women's Volleyball Championship.

    5. The AVCA actively prepares and develops clinics, seminars and workshops for the professional development of its constituency.

    6. The AVCA promotes and increases the media exposure of volleyball. The founding of the U.S. Volleyball Media Association, in cooperation with USA Volleyball, is a major step toward involving media in its own network. In addition, the AVCA is a member of the College Sports Information Directors of America and delivers presentations to that group.

    7. The AVCA has written a National Volleyball Statistics Manual & Video and has been the primary force in developing a consistent method of compiling volleyball statistics.

    8. Until 1994, the AVCA compiled and publicized all individual and team statistical information for every Division I school on a weekly basis and monthly for every Division II, III and NAIA school throughout the women's season. Upon compilation of statistics by the NCAA in 1994, the AVCA ceased this activity except for the NAIA.

    9. The AVCA coordinates the polling of coaches weekly for ranking of the Top 25 teams in Division I; the Top 25 in Division II; the Top 15 in Division III and Division I men's; and the Top 10 in Division III men's volleyball. The Division I men's and women's polls are carried by USA TODAY. The other polls are carried by the AP Sports Stats Wire and major papers.

    10. The AVCA administered the National Invitational Volleyball Championship, a 20-team Division I championship for institutions that were not selected to the NCAA championship. Through close contacts with all conference offices, the NIVC became a premier event for up and coming teams.

Other Educational Resources Available

The American Volleyball Coaches Association, in conjunction with USA Volleyball, the National Governing Body for the sport in the United States, is proud to offer a number of excellent educational publications through Volleyball Informational Products, a joint program of the two organizations

In addition to *The Best of Coaching Volleyball, Book Three: The Related Elements of the Game*, the following educational publications are also available:

- *The AVCA Volleyball Handbook*
- *The Best of Coaching Volleyball, Book One: The Basic Elements of the Game*
- *The Best of Coaching Volleyball, Book Two: The Advanced Elements of the Game*
- *Cadre Collection Volume II*
- *The Coaches Guide to Beginning Volleyball Programs*
- *Coaching Volleyball Successfully*
- *Critical Thinking on Setter Development*
- *Pass, Set, Crush*
- *Rookie Coaches Guide*
- *The Science of Coaching Volleyball*
- *Strength Training and Conditioning for Volleyball*

Also, the following periodicals are available:
American Volleyball (official AVCA newsletter, 12 issues per year)
Coaching Volleyball (official AVCA technical journal, six issues per year)
Power Tips (high school/junior drill bulletin, 12 issues per year)
Volleyball USA (USA Volleyball official magazine, four issues per year)

Finally, there is also an extensive video library available. The videos included in the collection explore all aspects of volleyball at levels ranging from beginner to advanced. Some of the nation's finest volleyball coaches provide expert technical direction.

For more information on any of these educational resource materials, please contact Volleyball Informational Products at 1-800-275-8782.